GENDER *and* POLITICS
in
NAYANTARA SAHGAL

GENDER *and* POLITICS
in
NAYANTARA SAHGAL

RACHEL BARI

PARTRIDGE
A Penguin Random House Company

To order additional copies of this book, contact
Partridge India
000 800 10062 62
orders.india@partridgepublishing.com

www.partridgepublishing.com/india

Contents

Preface ix

I   Introduction.. 1
     Why the foray into history? 4
     Establishing home as an archival material 22

II   The Beginnings.. 26
     Life as Nayantara sees it: Fiction,
     history and gender...35

III Change and Nayantara Sahgal 59
     Sahgal's Feminist Priorities *Rich Like Us:*........ 64

IV   Politics and Tradition 85
     Tradition-Modernity and Personal
     Relationships:... 88
     Nayantara – the insider participant 91

V   Towards A Conclusion 99

Bibliography...105

I dedicate this

To my husband Syed A. Bari and my son Rayhaan Bari
for understanding that every exit of mine
was an entrance somewhere.

Preface

This work derives from a research project that I worked on in 2014 funded by the University Grants Commission, New Delhi. Gender has always been a compelling area of interest, so also has been fiction and history. I am no student of history but in today's world of interdisciplinary studies, can one remain unaffected by this process of making history? There has been scholarship in this area for quite some time now and I am not perhaps breaking ground, but this work adds to the existing one. I am indebted to many scholars who have worked in this ever expanding area of research and have had the opportunity to not only read them but to generously borrow from their ideologies which made my germinating ideas more meaningful and fulfilling to me as a researcher. I have not scrutinsed and bear no scholarship in history but my reading of history takes place through different genres: poetry, fiction, short story, a film, an event in society or even in the way people behave. This is contemporary for me and it is through this contemporaneity that I seek answers from the past and the changes that have occurred, might have occurred or still can occur. If this is a notion unacceptable to traditional historians, then maybe I just cannot help it. History stares at me from almost everywhere and stories build through them. Whether we would want to call it historical fiction or fictionalized history is a debate, I leave to more learned scholars. I will not enter it though I have made a hurried entrance and exit from it!

More interesting to me has been the involvement that I have had with women and history which later took turns to become feminist historiography and much later gendered history. I have had a hurried entrance there too! Since my background, call it reading or training (though I still don't know how one can be trained in literature unless you would want to make it a scientific discipline, which unfortunately is happening now) has been in teaching gender/feminism and finding it difficult to reach the students at some level, I have dug deeper. I feel like an actor in the entire process of teaching and learning. So have many others, through other professions and interests. Why is it that none is represented? What are we missing? Why is it that I do not know about cats and dogs and horses and birds as part of a historical process? Why do writers write about it and it does not get included in history? Except for a few famous horses mentioned in history, what happened to the numerous experiences we have had with animals, which changed or charged our behavior with differences? What were our relationships? With men, with women, with animals, with nature etc. Is that why we have eco history, eco feminism? We build houses, homes: in fiction, these speak, in history it is silent. The graffiti on walls leave a different trail, the walls themselves tell a different story. Food tells a different story. If these stories do not whisper a tale, where else do

I have to look for tales? In rigid archives which are as stiff as the men who were commissioned to write it? There I do not find a tale, I find gaping holes staring at me with a cry to fill it. What do I fill it with and where do I find it from? If not literature and various other experiences that one goes through in life, where else? In pots and pans, in kitchens and cooking, in living rooms and hushed conversations history takes shape. If we ignore it, we ignore life. Perhaps from this arises the reason for taking a renewed look at archives.

Archive, is the way life unfolds through stories in Sahgal's fiction. I have used her discursive writings without at times acknowledging it as discursive. Without it, the idea of trying to read gendered history into her works would have been futile.

The work has attempted to read Sahgal as a writer of fiction, where fiction can be seen as an important chronicle of the past events, though personal. Being a gendered study of her fiction, it has emphasized gendered relationships in her works. It has accomplished not only aspects of women's history but also feminist history.

I owe it to the University Grants Commission of India for having funded this research project, Kuvempu University of Karnataka for having given me an opportunity to complete this work and the Central University of Gujarat for helping me publish this with additions and modifications.

To two people I owe an immense gratitude. My husband Syed A. Bari, presently the Vice Chancellor of the Central University of Gujarat, Gandhinagar, Gujarat and my son

Rayhaan Bari who have understood my compulsions, my interests, my commitments and many a time, my stubbornness in getting this work done. They have mentored me, supported me and restored my confidence and belief in the notion that conditioning need not always be patriarchal, it can provide a new model in building a new mindset. A line so close to what I feel and would like to communicate is from Tom Stoppard's *Rosencrantz and Guildenstern are Dead* which I use in my dedication to them. Thank you both for being what you are. And thank you Ishmeet for the patience in clicking the photograph. You believed.

RACHEL BARI

Introduction

I am a novelist and a political journalist. My novels have a political background or political ambiance. I didn't plan it that way—I was dealing with people and situations—but looking back, each one seems to reflect the hopes and fears the political scene held out to us at the time.

I have a very strong emotional as well as intellectual attachment to my roots ... I have certainly been plagued with wondering from time to time why I was born and what I'm doing here and why I haven't had to worry about my next meal when millions live lives of anxiety and drudgery. And then there is the problem of evil and pain. At times all that abstract conjecture has become very personal, with the need to atone for the terrible things people do to each other. Some of these matters fell into place for me when I gave up the struggle to be an atheist. Atheism—or agnosticism—is my general family background, but I am. a believer to the marrow of my bones, and much has become clearer to me since I faced the fact.

I see myself as both novelist and journalist. In the course of a lifetime one is many things, fiction is my abiding love, but I need to express myself on vital political issues. Political and social forces shape our lives. How can we be unaware of them? I believe there is a "poetics of engagement" where commitment and aesthetics meet and give each other beauty and power.[1]

Born in into a very politically active family, Nayantara Sahgal's fiction did not escape the volatile atmosphere in which she lived. Her fiction permeates with the charged political atmosphere of the post independent era when India was emerging from the shadows of colonialism and trying to carve out an identity for herself. Her people were caught and saddled in the throes of a country in momentum. Nayantara Sahgal records those moments and it is the study of those moments which brings in the much needed change in the way history is read.

Nayantara Sahgal's nine novels and eight works of non-fiction deal with India's elite responding to the crises engendered by political change. It is also important to know that she was one of the first woman Indian writers in English to receive wide recognition. Being a member of the Nehru-Gandhi family and second of the three daughters

---

[1] http://biography.jrank.org/pages/4707/Sahgal-Nayantara-Pandit.html

born to Nehru's 's sister, Vijayalakshmi Pandit, she had close access to the political climate brewing in the country.

Born on May 10, 1927 into one of India's most prominent political families, with her mother Vijayalakshmi Pandit as India's first ambassador to the U.N., her uncle Jawaharlal Nehru as India's first Prime Minister, and her first cousin, Indira Gandhi as India's third Prime Minister, it is not surprising that politics and history inspire and underlie much of her writing. Beginning with her memoir *Prison and Chocolate Cake*, which was published in 1954, Sahgal authored other political writings - *The Freedom Movement in India* and *Indira Gandhi, Her Road to Power* - along with a collection of essays, *Point of view: a personal response to life, literature and politics.*

Her fiction brings out her feminist concerns seeking independent existence of women. She sees women as victims of conventional Indian society engaged in their quest for identity. In her last novel *Mistaken Identity* her concept of emancipation reaches its pinnacle where her female character is an out-and-out rebel.

Nayantara Sahgal served as an advisor to Sahitya Akademi's Board for English from 1972 to 1975. She was a member of Verghese Committee for Autonomy to Radio & TV in 1977-78. In 1978, she was member of the Indian delegation to U.N. General Assembly. She has also held the post of Vice-President of People's Union for Civil Liberties.

She received the Sinclair Prize (Britain) for fiction in 1985, Sahitya Akademi Award in 1986, and Commonwealth

Writers Award (Eurasia) in 1987. She was also a Fellow of the Woodrow Wilson International Centre for Scholars, Washington from 1981 to 1982. She was awarded the 1986 Sahitya Akademi Award for English, for her novel, *Rich Like Us* (1985), by the Sahitya Akademi, India's National Academy of Letters. And very recently in 2015 she returned her Akademi Award in protest of the growing intolerance of differences in community and ideology in India with many other writers following suit.

Educated in the United States at Wellesley College (B.A., 1947), she was well acquainted with Indian aristocracy. Her fiction was often set between personal conflict amid Indian political crises.

The contrast between the idealism at the beginning of India's independence and the moral decline of post-Nehru India that is particularly evident in *A Situation in New Delhi* (1977) recurs in other novels as *Rich like Us* (1985), which confront civil disorder, corruption, and oppression while detailing the internal conflicts in a businessman's family. Two of Sahgal's later novels, *Plans for Departure* (1985) and *Mistaken Identity* (1988), are set in colonial India. Her works of nonfiction include *Relationship, Extracts from a Correspondence* (1994) and *Point of View: A Personal Response to Life, Literature, and Politics* (1997).

Why the foray into history?

Since the 1970's when women's history entered the academia, the endeavour to read history from an "other" point of view has always been a need. It was not an agenda but a need. And the need like any other feminist endeavour was to be visible in an otherwise crowded world where women, their work, their presence and their thoughts were always rendered invisible. And this invisibility has taken place in different ways. What we now know and classify as woman's history, gendered history or feminist history is a clear indication that this visibility that women claimed has indeed happened and is happening in different dimensions.

History has to be Herstory if a complete picture has to emerge. Traditional historians have always debunked this concept because feminist history and its methodology is something that they do not trust because its variables are just that: variables. How do you interpret history with variables? And highly unstable ones at that! Only facts can generate true history because one way of reading and understanding history is through data, and data has to be realistic, measured and concrete.

Without going into scholarly attempts to understand and define history, for I am no historian, I would want to understand history as a study of past events and the work of historians is to study this past and produce scholarship on this. It sounds simple at this juncture, but is not really so. Kent (1) questions the simplicity of this statement and asks whether producing scholarship about the past is a simple exercise? She contends that the 'past' is not static, stable, nor stagnant. There is no 'past' out there just waiting for us to faithfully reproduce it, even if we had all the time and all the resources in the world to do so. (Kent, 1)

And as any historian knows, the past is interpreted and reconstructed. And this interpretation and reconstruction is on the basis of the type of questions that the historian asks of it at a particular point of time and obviously these questions change over time.

When questions are asked – there is always the question of influence and agency. What questions are asked, who asks them and why? And most important – what or who is left out?

> The answers to their queries determine what our histories look like, and because the queries and the answers they yield themselves change over time, history itself has a history (Kent I)

To further the argument by Kent, this makes one feel that history is subjective. If that is so then one has nothing to be disgruntled about. Kent however reminds us that any subject is a discipline and if it is so then there are rules and regulations to be followed. There must be an "... ordering of knowledge"(Kent 2) that a researcher must adhere to. One must be careful in using evidence and contextualizing it. Not everybody could be a historian for it entails an enormous responsibility. Evidence gives rise to ideas and it is then we enter the very abstract world of theory.

A look at the differences of gendered history, women's history and feminist is perhaps the need of the hour, yet an inventory is unwarranted. But a short detour would perhaps help.

I would not want to dwell much over the intricacies of theory here, but to bring in a sense of discipline, I shall briefly run through the differences.

Women's history studies women as *subjects* largely as a result of the efforts of the feminist movement of the 1970's. There was a search for a woman's past, to make her a subject of the historical process. The search for the woman's past rested on two assumptions according to Kent, one - that if women were to be regarded as historical actors, historians would have to regard them as partaking of a collective identity and secondly women shared a collective set of experiences on the basis of which they formed a collective identity. (2012,50) This aspect is debatable because the experiences of women vary over cultures and races, nevertheless women in a given historical time, in a particular location and culture perhaps do share a collective set of experiences. The partition experience of women in India could be cited as an instance. They suffered because of their sex and this was common to all women across all religions. Here they shared a common oppression.

Women's history was largely compensatory and contributory.[2] However Jill Matthews feels that "...these histories... treated women according to masculine standards of significance: they mostly described what men of the past told women to do, what men of the past thought women ought to be ..."(147)[3]

---

[2] Gerda Lerner, "Placing women in History: Definitions and Challenges', *Feminist Studies,* Vol.3 Nos 1/2 Fall 1975, 5 - 14

[3] *Feminist History Labour History, No.50 (may 1986) 147 - 153*

Thus women acted as men and thought as men and how men wanted women to think. Thus "women were also there..." [4] as the case would be, this kind of contributory history was criticized by feminist historians. There was a need to do something different. The challenge "...was not just to add women to the standard canon...", "...plug the gap "etc but to "...do over the whole enterprise".[5] Women's history adds women to the standard categories of historical analysis and deals with them in those terms. For instance when a feminist historian adds women to "labour", she does not just work on women and labour but the whole meaning of labour is debated and worked out. If she adds women to politics, then the whole meaning of politics is worked out. Terms means differently to men and women.

Having researched and worked it out, Matthews gives us certain guidelines.[6] Since then the concept of gendered history has come a long way.

Gendered History on the other hand studies the "... relationship of women to men in the context of various societies, paying particular attention to the interplay of male and female identities". (Kent 2012 49) Both use subjects and methods which overlap each other. And at no point of time do we value one over the other for they are complementary to each other and historically linked. Gendered history depends very heavily on women's history

---

[4] Gerda Learner as in note I
[5] Jill Matthews as in note 2
[6] For information on the guidelines see Jill Matthews as in note 1 and 2

for the material it analyses and women's history would be incomplete information if it did not put the relationships in a gendered perspective.

It is understood that neither woman's culture nor the social history approach could rewrite conventional history. [7] Joan Scott suggested that feminist historians who hoped to transform history as a practice should incorporate 'gender' into their studies, an analytic category that derived from and expanded upon the abundance of studies already produced by historians of women.[8]

Scott, we[9] are told was not the first to introduce the concept of gender. Joan Kelly and Natalie Zemon Davis in the 1970's had argued that rather than try to study women in isolation from men, women historians needed to study them in relation to men. Davis's quote would be interesting here.

> ...we should be interested in the history of both women and men...we should not be working only on the subjected sex...Our goal is to understand the significance of the sexes...to discover the range in sex roles and in sexual symbolism in different societies and periods, to find out what meaning they had and how they functioned to maintain the social order or to promote its change" (Women's history 90)

---

[7] For explanation see Kent 53.
[8] Joan Wallach Scott, "Women In History: The Modern Period, No 101 (Nov 1983) 141-157 OUP www.jstor.org/stable/650673
[9] Susan Kingsley Kent *Gender and History* pp 53-54

Interestingly the word 'gender' is not used here.

Gendered history is not just history of women; it is an integral part but not the whole focus. "...Gender history incorporates both women and men, masculinity and femininity and sexual difference generally, it places men and women in relation to each other. (Kent 4)

Underlying gender history is the conviction that we now know that gender is not natural nor innocent and what societies have thought and envisioned about gender has changed. These constructions have been accepted but they have also been resisted. Gender has been appropriated by power.

Gendered history is a terminology that needs elaboration. These two terms which are a discipline by themselves, when brought together collide with great intensity.

Gender, apart from the meanings generated also stressed the relational aspect of normative definitions of femininity. Those who worried that women's studies scholarship focused too narrowly and separately on women used the term "gender" to introduce a relational notion into our analytic vocabulary. According to this view, women and men were defined in terms of one another, and no understanding of either could be achieved by entirely separate study. Thus Natalie Davis suggested in 1975, "It seems to me that we should be interested in the history of both women and men, that we should not be working only on the subjected sex any more than an historian of class can focus entirely on peasants. Our goal is to understand the significance of the sexes, of gender groups in the historical past. Our goal is to discover the range in sex roles and in sexual symbolism in different societies and periods, to find out what meaning they had and how they functioned to maintain the social order or to promote its c h a n g e." [10]

In addition, and perhaps most important, "gender" was a term offered by those who claimed that women's scholarship would fundamentally transform disciplinary paradigms. Feminist scholars pointed out early on that the study of women would not only add new subject matter but would also force a critical re-examination of the premises and standards of existing scholarly work. "We are learning," wrote three feminist historians, "...that the writing of women into history necessarily involves redefining and enlarging traditional notions of historical significance, to encompass personal, subjective experience as well as public and political activities. It is not too much to suggest that however hesitant the actual beginning, such a methodology implies not only a new history of women, but also a new history."[11]

The way in which this new history would both include and account for women's experience rested on the extent to which gender could be developed as a category of analysis. Here the analogies to class (and race) were explicit: indeed,

---

[10] Natalie Zemonn Davis, "Women's History in Transition: The European Case Feminist Studies 3 Winter 1975-76 90.

[11] Ann D Jordan, Mari Jo Bhule and Nancy Shrom Dye, "The Problem of Women's History" in Bernice Carroll Ed *Liberating Women's History*, Urbana III 1976 89

the most politically inclusive of scholars of women's studies regularly invoked all three categories as crucial to the writing of a new history.[12]

Can Feminist Historiography be seen as the tension between history and history writing? This seems to be the most appropriate point to begin with. I base my argument on Cheryl Glenn's *Comment: Truth, Lies, and Method: Revisiting Feminist Historiography*[13]. The contention of Glenn as she says has never been to supplant the master narrative with a "mater" narrative, but bring in deeply contextualized narratives for a fuller, richer and different picture into focus. (388) It is interesting to note that for Glenn the text of history writing initiates a play between the object under study and the discourse performing the analysis. (ibid 388)

What is the past to us? Does it give us identification or does it negate our sense of identity? Or "...can this relationship be negotiated through hermeneutical detours."? [14] Is feminist historiography yet another methodology? Our relationship to our past is unique in this sense that it is a lived experience and it is through this experience that history is to be understood and explained. Our historical inquiries thus

---

[12] Joan Kelly "The Double Vision of Feminist Theory" in *Women, History and Feminist Theory*, Chicago 1984 51-64

[13] College English, Volume 62, number 3, January 2000 387-389 accessed on 28.9.2012 07.20

[14] Understanding Feminist Historiography Reviewed Work(s) Economic and Political Weekly Vol 25, No 31 (Aug 4 1990) pp 1735-1736 http://www.jstor.org/stable/4396591 accessed 28.9.2012 07.12

become relevant and necessary. Feminist historiography is premised on this understanding. (Ibid) In other words, as Jill Mathews says "...it is not the subject matter but how it is handled which determines feminist history, whereas subject matter is central to women's history."(Feminist History 150) and more importantly "What is central to feminist history is the recognition of gender relations as a major power dynamic within history" (Ibid)

It is indeed important to understand that the distinction/ difference between women's and feminist history is not on the subject matter but on approach. It challenges stereotypical notions of the nature of women and tends to look at specific circumstances, the social forces affecting the conditions and patterns of their lives.

What are the changing patterns and organisations of power and resistance that constituted the specific and changing definitions and self-definitions of women?

In today's world of interdisciplinary studies, being a student of just literature is impossible. One crosses boundaries all the time in pursuit of new knowledge. While reading Nayantara Sahgal, I kept crossing boundaries all the time. I could not read her just as another writer who wrote fiction and strict compartmentalization was not possible in this particular area because often they kept colliding and intermingling.

Having said that let me attempt to discuss these two issues. First, Gender. To a large extent, I am deeply indebted to Susan Kinglsey Kent. For a person who was averse to theory, she opened up a spectacular world of theory closely related to gender. Things feel into place when I started reading Kent's *Gender and History*.[15]

What is Gender? We remember Stoller's "Sex is biological, gender is cultural" and we think gender to be socially and culturally constructed. Apart from theories of gender which have been given to us, by philosophers, theoreticians, feminists etc, it is interesting to note that at a practical level, gender operates everywhere and nowhere. Ideas about gender, in other words, about male and female, men and women, masculine and feminine operate everywhere in the lives that we live. Because it is everywhere we believe it to be natural, i.e, they are derived from nature. However we have been hearing about gender for the past hundreds of years and if everything else has changed, hasn't gender? Does it not mean that gender itself has a history? In other words, "...these have a history; they change over time and vary by geographic or cultural contexts. They aren't natural. We make them – we construct them..." (Kent 3)

Gender construction is an ongoing process. It does not stop at a particular time or at a particular geographical area. It is a part of the political process at work in the society and is always at work to" "...further a particular, political, cultural, economic or social agenda."(Kent 3)

Gender, as we all know is always embedded in a power relationship. If this is so then this is neither natural nor

---

[15] Susan Kingsley Kent *Gender and History* Palgrave Macmillan 2012.

neutral. If this is neither natural nor neutral then it means that there is a conflict and if there is a conflict then it has two sides. But when we think of gender, we think only of women, as though gender is an offshoot of the study of feminism. Men are rarely seen as 'gendered creatures. However things have changed with studies on masculinities. Today we realize that men are also gendered.

Joan Scott says that gender consists of knowledge that societies formulate, the understandings that various cultures produce about sexual difference, differences in the physical, mental, moral and emotional complexions of men and women that are purported to come from nature and that prescribe their proper role and activities. Kent has argued that the production of knowledge about gender itself has a history. Thus it means that this knowledge which is constructed is not true or total. Whatever is constructed is disseminated through various institutions, political and religious outfits etc., One must also remember that the use of gender and the knowledge created about sexual difference is through the relationship of power.

The other area is the dichotomy between fiction and history. What place fiction has in locating real time gendered relations in the society of the times is perhaps a question which has time and again been a query with traditional historians. Fiction is just that: Fiction. The dictionary meaning of fiction (n) is not very encouraging either.

> 'Something invented by the imagination or feigned'
> 'An assumption of a possibility as a fact irrespective of the question of its truth'

'useful illusion or pretense'
'The action of feigning or of creating with the imagination'

Merriam-Webster

The fact/fiction dichotomy has been there for some time now. Not going to details again, traversing the path briefly is in order.

Speaking about historical fiction, Hayden White, a leading critic claims that the surge in popularity of historical fiction and the novel form in the nineteenth century caused historians to seek recognition of their field as "a serious "science" (Rethinking History 149). Historians believed that, to be scientific, historical studies had to cut ties with any form of artistic writing or imaginative literature, especially the romantic novel. German historian Leopold von Ranke "anathematized" the historical novel virtually from its first appearance in Scott's *Waverley* in 1814. Hayden White argues that Ranke and others after him wrote history as narrative while eschewing the use of imagination and invention that were "exiled into the domain of 'fiction'" (149-150).

Early critics in the nineteenth century questioned the value of historical fiction. Georg Lukács, in his much-cited *The Historical Novel*, first published in 1937, was concerned with the social aspect of the historical novel and its capacity to portray the lives of its protagonists. Through its attention to the detail of minor events, this way of writing was better at highlighting the social aspects than the greater moments of history. Lukács argues that the historical novel should focus on the "poetic awakening" of those who participated in great historical events rather than the events themselves (42). The reader should be able to experience first-hand "the social and human motives which led men to think, feel and act just as they did in historical reality" (ibid). Through historical fiction, the reader is thus able to gain a greater understanding of a specific period and why people acted as they did.

In contrast, historian and author of three books on history and three novels, Richard Slotkin, argues that the historical novel can recount the past as accurately as history, because it should involve similar research methods and critical interpretation of the data (225).. In its search for "poetic truth," the novel tries to create a sense of what the past was, without necessarily adhering to all the factual details and by eliminating facts not essential to the story (Slotkin 225).

For Hayden White, the difference between factual and fictional discourse, is that one is occupied by what is "true" and the other by what is "real" (147).

Historical documents may provide a basis for a "true account of the world" in a certain time and place, but they are limited in their capacity to act as a foundation for the exploration of all aspects of "reality." To quote White himself

> The rest of the real, after we have said what we can assert be true about it, would not be everything and anything we could imagine about it. The real would consist of everything that can be truthfully said about its actuality plus everything that can

be truthfully said about what it could possibly be. (ibid)

White's main point is that both history and fiction are interpretative by nature. Historians interpret given evidence from a subjective viewpoint and this means that it cannot be unbiased. Both fiction and history are narratives, and "*anyone* who writes a narrative is fictionalizing," according to Keith Jenkins (cited in Southgate 32).

The novelist and historian find meaning through their own interpretation of the known record (Brown) to produce stories that are entertaining and structured. Moreover, historians often reach conflicting conclusions in their translations of the same archival documents, which can lead to disputes.

The historian's purpose differs from that of the novelist. Historians examine the historical record in fine detail in an attempt to understand its complexities, and through footnoting explain and lend authority to their findings. The novelist on the other hand, uses their imagination to create personalities and plot and can leave out important details; the novelist achieves authenticity through detailed description of setting, customs, culture, buildings and so on (Brown).

Nevertheless, the main task of both history and historical fiction is to represent the past to a reader in the present; this "shared concern with the construction of meaning through narrative" is a major component in the long-lasting, close relationship between fiction and history (Southgate 19).

Attitudes towards the line drawn between fiction and history are changing as more and more critics and theorists explore the area where the two genres intersect. Historian John Demos argues that with the passing of time, this distinction "seems less a boundary than a borderland of surprising width and variegated topography" (Afterword: 329).While some historians are now willing to investigate the wide area where the two genres overlap, this approach remains a concern for traditionalists.

Historians face a crisis as they try to come to terms with the unprecedented questioning of the validity of history's claim to accuracy in recounting the past. In the words of Jenkins et al., "'history' *per se* wobbles" as it experiences a period of uncertainty and challenge; the field is "much changed and deeply contested," as historians seek to understand the meaning of history itself (6).

White argues that the crisis in historical studies is due to historians having failed to live up to their nineteenth century expectations of history being recognized as a science (149). This kind of historiography has denied itself access to aesthetic writing and the imaginary, while it has also cut any links it had "to what was most creative in the real sciences it sought half-heartedly to emulate" (ibid). Furthering White's argument, historian Robert Rosenstone states that the claims of historians to be the sole guardians of historical truth now seem outdated in the light of accumulated knowledge. The once impregnable position of the historian is no longer tenable because:

> We know too much about framing images and stories, too much about narrative, too much about

the problematics of causality, too much about the subjectivity of perception, too much about our own cultural imperatives and biases, too much about the disjuncture between language and the world it purports to describe to believe we can actually capture the world of the past on the page. (Rosenstone 12)

While the archive confers credibility on history, it does not confer the right to historians to claim it as *the* truth (Southgate 6); there are many possible versions of the past, which can be presented to us in any number of ways as history (Jenkins et al. 1).And this is a major challenge for historians

Public interest in history has grown over the years. Rosenstone laments the fact that historians, despite this attraction to the past, have failed to stir public interest in their own writings. While works of history have their strengths, they target a specific, extremely limited audience in an outdated format (17). They have forgotten the fact that, in the words of White, "the conjuring up of the past requires art as well as information" (149).

However, those historians who do write outside the limits of traditional history can attract criticism. Historian Richard Current argues that if writers of history and biography try to be more effective through literary considerations, they sometimes lose their objectivity and authenticity. While it is acceptable to seek to write with clarity and force, it is out of the question to present "occasional scenes in lifelike detail" in the manner of a novelist. Modern-day historians are contesting this viewpoint as they analyse the nature and role of their writings, with some turning to historical fiction as an alternative mode of expression.

Our only way of grasping our history or what has happened to us, and what determines what we are now and where we are now—the only way of really coming to terms with that is by people's entering into it in their imagination, not by the world of facts, but by being there. And the only thing really which puts you there in that kind of way is fiction.

From this point of view, novel plays an important role in our culture because it allows people to interact with the past in a meaningful way, something factual writing struggles to do. McKenna recognizes that history is present in fiction and that history can contain fiction, but they should not be confused.

The trouble between history and fiction will continue for some time as traditional historians are bent on keeping faith with the tenets of their nineteenth century predecessors by defending history from the insurgence of fiction. While history and fiction share a common purpose in presenting the past, the novel deals with what is "real" and can tell the past as accurately or even in a more plausible way than history, which deals with what is "true". Many historians recognize the need for change in the way they present their work, but as they have often doubted the worth of historical fiction, they are wary of the genre and the narrative techniques it employs. Those historians who do make an attempt to write differently have often been criticized by traditionalists.

The scenario that emerges is of two fields that are still struggling to clarify a number of important issues concerning the nature of both fiction and historiographical writing, and the role they play in portraying the past.

It is increasingly apparent now that the boundaries are merging, though problems exist. Nayantara's writing does not fall into the category of historical fiction, but history can be discerned through her writing and this is important data in terms of feminist historiography for garnering information about gendered relationships.

Establishing home as an archival material

Women's writing has always been "home centered" and it is precisely because of this that not much interest is generated for their writing. The criticism has always been that they do not talk about the "larger issues" of life and hence the focus and canvas is always limited and small. Perceptions have changed today. Scholarly works have put "home" at the center to probe deep into the gendered aspects of women's writing. Hence very importantly home becomes an archive. Explaining this Burton says

> What counts as an archive? Can private memories of home serve as political history? What do we make of the histories that domestic interiors, once concrete and now perhaps crumbling or even disappeared, have the capacity to yield? And, given women's vexed relationship to the kinds of history that archives typically house, what does it mean to say that home

> can and should be seen not simply as a dwelling place
> for women's memory but as one of the foundations of
> history – history conceived of, that is, as a narrative,
> a practice, and a site of desire?"(2003 4)

It was essential to use the quotation in full here for it is very significant. Women writers have had to face enormous challenges in their writing career. If we were to go back to 1929 and remember Virginia Woolf's *A Room Of One's Own*, we would understand those challenges. Then it was a demand for 'money' and 'space' for creativity. Today that creative space is not deemed important. That 'space' is private and domestic and with the kind of men's traditions available for women in writing, it is but natural that this domestic space is deemed valueless. How else would a woman express herself if not through the domestic sphere? Where else would she play out her drama of life if not at home? And how would she weave out her stories and ideas except through memories? Armed with these weapons of identity, today women's writing has found its way into the domains of history, wanting to make a difference: difference in the way that women are perceived and the way they have contributed. They question the process and the access to knowledge and the production of that knowledge.

The question would be can we use memories of home in order to claim a place in history at the intersection of the private and the public, the personal and the political, the national and post-colonial. The home and the house are central to women's identities, social and cultural because it is through the space called home that women experience their identities. But this would limit the importance of women to either a space called home or an aspect called memory.

The domestic space is an archival source. Women construct their own histories through which they record their living as Indian women in the times they live, here the post independent context. Can the domestic scene be used not only for commemoration but also critique the present scenario that they live in? Having asked that let us go back to archives. Archive is used in two ways

1. Conventional, disciplinary meaning – a source of evidence from which each woman produced historical accounts of life in post-independent India.

2. Fiction/Narrative as an enduring site of historical evidence and historiographical opportunity.

In such a situation, narratives can serve as evidence of individual lives vis-a-vis of women in post independent India and also their memories of home itself become archival material. The word archive derives from the Greek word arkheion, which means house, residence, domicile of the archon (Chief Magistrate) and that this dwelling place marks the liminal space between public and private – those typically gendered domains as the characteristic features of critical historical consciousness. [16]

Women live in structurally gendered locations, the reason perhaps for the cult of domesticity to have thrived. It is through the home that they have retained and reinforced not only memories of their own identities but also their

---

[16] Derrida. *Archive Fever*. Chicago: University of Chicago Press, 1995 p2

lived in experience. As Burton says "Critical analyses of home that do not wish to either essentialize or romanticize its allegorical power must ...be attentive to the specific languages, metaphors and tropes through which it is articulated by historical subjects." (2003 6)

The memories of home that a woman enshrines in a narrative act ought to be seen as an archive, because it is through this that a variety of counter histories of colonial modernity can be discerned. Burton further emphasizes "...the importance of home as both a material archive for history and a very real political figure in an extended moment of historical crisis". (2003 5)

She further argues that the dynamic relationship between what are deemed discourses and what are designated material realities – between history and home – one can fully appreciate them as sites which are mutually constitutive of cultural knowledge and political desire. It is therefore easier to understand discourse and reality not as opposing domains but as a vast interdependent archive: a space where contests over colonial domination can be discerned and historicised. (Burton 2003 6)

Women and gender are the analytical categories at the heart of this critical approach. It is interesting to note that the domain that the home houses has its boundaries drawn for it by the larger culture as well as by the political economies of race, nation, sexuality and empire that shape it.

The Beginnings

It is but appropriate to begin this analysis with Sahgal's *Prison and Chocolate Cake* because it is from here that we begin to discern traditions of feminine writing and an account of how she saw her life and the path that it was going to take. She says "If I write haphazardly, it is because I describe events as I remember them and not necessarily in the order in which it occurred." (Preface vii) Further she says that "… the pattern forms in its own way as the pieces are located, and not in the neat methodological way desired (Preface vii)

At the time she was writing, Gandhiji's name was history and she tries to "…recapture a little of that fading atmosphere." (vii) This is significant because it is here that memory intrudes. The question could be can the past be captured "factually"? And <u>what</u> and <u>how</u> does she try to recapture?

She and her sister Lekha are to be sent to America for higher studies and their parents are in jail. Her mother is released due to her illness and they prepare to meet their father. But before that Nayantara records the events of seeing her father in prison. She cries in "misery" and "helpless anger" but her father tells her "We mustn't let these people see us cry..." (Preface x) To Nayantara her father was the "handsomest, the most lovable, kind and understanding person I knew, the human being nearest my heart and the ones whose opinion I most respected." (x) She remembers her parents as never having inflicted advice on them and they had grown up making their own choices and decisions. She speaks about their faith and trust in them as children, they were neither men nor women, they were just children.

An account of their travel on the ship bound to America reveals the inherent curiosity of the girls, Lekha and Nayantara, for life. They had none of the hesitation of the average girl at that age and mingled with everyone on board without prejudice. It would not be wrong to deduce that the influence of the parents on the psyche of the girls was quite profound. Nayantara recalls that her father was "proud and indulgent... (and) He firmly believed that girls should have essentially the same type of upbringing as boys" (Prison 31) However if this was true of Nayantara's family it wasn't so in the case of Uttar Pradesh where she says "In a country where education, opportunities and freedom given to boys are far greater than those allowed to girls, his was a rare attitude." (31) Though tolerant, what aroused his fiery temper was what he called the "purdah mentality", in other words the suppression or seclusion of women or denial of privileges. Historically, she says that women in Western India had enjoyed a greater amount of freedom than women in the North.

Nayantara speaks about her great grandmother Gopika, who bore eight sons and five daughters and had the "distinction" of having committed Suttee! The author does not speak about it as oppression, neither is the birth of 8 sons and 5 daughters. This is memory and this memory is interspersed with the memory of the community in which she lived. She does not speak about this in terms of oppression or suppression. It is seen as a distinction. Here then, is the function of memory, who remembers and how they remember is important. It is also essential to know what link triggers off this piece of knowledge. The context is of knowing the Indian childhood and Nayantara remembers this because this is so different from what happens in the West.

One gets a vivid picture of life lived by the Pandits, their food, their socializing and their holiday retreats at Khali. One also get a vivid and intimate picture of Jawaharlal, as seen by the throngs of humanity when they would come to Anand bhawan to see him as they had gone to bathe in the confluence of the two river, the Ganga and the Jamuna. (40)

In the 1936 elections in British India, Nayantara records for us the events which led to the victory of both her parents and of her mother's office, her work and what people thought about her. "To them her achievement was a natural thing... and U P received it with quiet confidence of a parent..." (67)

There are almost two pages devoted to women and their achievements, and the question is how do we see and read it today? Much has been said about women and their roles in India, as also the fact that the Indian woman got her right to vote much before her counterpart in America or Britain and we also know that there has been criticisms about Gandhi and the way he has treated women. There is also this problem of simplicity in the portrayal by a child of what she sees and how she sees. The grown up Nayantara attempts to retain that simplicity in the eyes of a child and since the time that this was written and today, a lot of research has taken place. Nevertheless the quest continues.

The subaltern picture in the book *Prison and Chocolate Cake* is what captures the eye. Nayantara, in all her childlike simplicity remembers all the people around her, European and Indian who played a supportive role in her growing up. Whether it was Hari the "untouchable" who had strayed into their house, or Sundar whom her father had called "Gaupo" or the gardener Rama who wept every time her father went jail, Bansi the day chowkidhar, they were all people who made a difference in their lives. So much so that when the gardener wept each time Pandit went to jail, he had felt "It was for men such as Rama...that India's freedom must be achieved, for it was to them, the simple, gentle people, that the soil of India really belonged." (83) It is through the eyes of a child narrator that one is able to discern the personality of Nehru through a different experience. That was a different India and Nehru is seen from al different lens.

Her character was also shaped by stories from history which throws light on history as read then, not as read today: truncated and distorted. Connected to Raksha Bandhan, is a story of Princess Kurnavathi of Chitoor who sent a rakhi to Humayun, the Moghul Emperor pleading for help to ward off the invader, who was a Muslim. Humayun heeds to her cry, gallops to Chitoor from Delhi but is too late. Chitoor is captured. Though the story is tragic, it reveals to us the times in which she lived and what shaped her character.(85) The building of a character in the times of Nayantara was an assimilation of the shared history of India and was not exclusive of the history which is a part of this culture. Much against what is happening in India today, Nayantara who was brought up without prejudice presents for us another side of the India, assimilating, tolerant and a leadership that did not attempt to divide on issues of caste, religion, region, identity.

What strikes the reader quite often in *Prison and Chocolate Cake* is the relationship between Papu (Nayantara's father) with his children as also Mamu's (Nehru) relationship with his nieces. Letters exchanged in 1939 about the imminent war and India's reluctance to join forces with England and the issue of Non-violence between Nayantara and her father give us a feel about their relationship which was based on respect of each other's ideas, however trivial they were. Twelve year old Nayantara's queries and confusions are answered patiently by Papu. There was never a question of treating Nayantara as a child and to hide her from what was taking place in the Indian scenario, nor was there the attitude of telling her "you are too young to know this". Nayanthara and her sisters grew up knowing about what India was going through and being actively engaged in the debate about what was right and wrong.

Here were two men actively engaged in the freedom struggle of India teaching their daughters the importance of being a part of the struggle and treating them as a mind and not as a body. They are given ample freedom to travel and learn whether it is in India or abroad. As specified in the beginning of this write up, this is perhaps a portion of the truth of gendered relationships in pre Independent India. That Nehru had time to 'play' and 'read' with his nieces is a piece of knowledge that we readers treasure. More so, when we see him shaping their minds, teaching them to think, reconsider and grow[17]. We get snippets of information which could have created an impact on the minds of these three girls for whom Nehru was obviously a very huge influence. In one such instance, Rita wants to know "Mamu, don't you get sick and tired of travelling around the country?" to which Nehru replies

"Tired, but not sick..."

And to Lekha's "...if life will ever be normal..." he says "... no use expecting life to be easy...should not be normal for intelligent human beings to spend all their time and energy killing each other off..."

and continues "...there is an advantage to living in abnormal times...of course if you are lacking in courage and poor in spirit...and I'm sure you three are not ...you won't see the advantage...They may be avenues full of risk and danger, but through them you can build a better world. There is adventure in living in abnormal times, and life without adventure would be a very dull affair...you must treat circumstances as an invitation to action..." (151)

---

[17] Read more in the chapter titled **About People** in *Prison and Chocolate Cake p 136 - 159*

Rita's earnest "I wish we could do something to help you...
all we do is go to school and have lessons and horrid things
like that...(151) to which he laughs wholeheartedly and says

> Those are just the things that will fit you for the
> future...They will give you the body that is strong,
> a mind that is as keen as the edge of a sword, and
> a character that is firm and steadfast and dedicated
> to high ideals (152)

They were brought up without restrictions physically
and mentally. It was as though their world did not have
gendered demarcations and there were no concessions for
being girls. This was not just the case with members of the
household. The very thought of bringing about freedom
for India permeated every thought and it was essential to
train every mind for that. If Nehru and Pandit had these
thoughts, women had it too. Sarojini Naidu who was a
frequent visitor to Anand Bhawan once asked Nayantara
"Would you rather be the most brilliant woman in the
world or the most beautiful?" to which the answer had been
"The most beautiful.." which was met with "Humph"... A
true woman! She doesn't care a fig for brains. I hope she'll
have more sense later on."(141) Beauty for a woman had a
place but not the only place; there were more important
things in life. Education was one among them. When
Nayantara and her sisters were being sent to America for
education, there were two kinds of views about it amongst
the friends of the Pandits. Mrs. Pandit received two books
at this time, one was *The Flowering of New England* with
the inscription "This will give you a better understanding
of the part of the United States to which your daughters are

going", and the "...other was a volume containing "statistics" of divorce, crime and venereal disease in the United states with a note attached pointing out the dangers of sending young girls unchaperoned to a foreign land".(160) There was encouragement and moral policing as well!

To Nayantara, education meant inside the class and outside the class. Exposure to different cultures enriched her perceptions of life. They had the leisure to "talk...attack and debate every conceivable subject" and also "think" and "argue and question" aspects which were taboo to girls/women in perhaps other sections in India.

The relationships between men and women were also one of mutual respect and understanding as is visible in many examples that are interspersed in the book. Standards were high, the goal was independence. There were many hurdles, money was not important, and life was uncertain. Acquaintances of the Pandits were amazed by this attitude and had said "It would be different if you had sons...sons could go their own ways and earn their own living...but you have daughters, each one of them has to be married. What will you give them when they marry? What will you give their husbands?" and Nayantara tells that her father treated them with "lighthearted disdain" and had said "I have ...given them an imperishable set of values which will last them all their lives...As for their husbands, if there are any men good enough for them they can be thankful that they will marry my daughters. I have nothing more precious to give" (173)

Her mother herself had at first been reluctant to send them away to America but her husband had said to "trust" them to make a life for themselves, to learn to live and have positive values. At a time in India, where education for women in India had to go through many hurdles, this is a different picture which emerges where men do not just encourage women's education but treat them on par with everything else. This was a time which demanded strength and women were strong. This was no time for weakness and women rose up in courage. This is nowhere better seen then during Gandhiji's death. Sarojini Naidu chides everybody. 'she says "What is all the snivelling about? Would you rather he had died of decrepit old age or indigestion? This was the only death great enough for him"(230) What better instance would one need of a different picture of India? Through Nayantara's *Prison and Chocolate Cake* we approach history from a different perspective.

As said earlier it is important to understand that the distinction/difference between women's and feminist history is not on the subject matter but on approach. It challenges stereotypical notions of the nature of women and tends to look at specific circumstances, the social forces affecting the conditions and patterns of their lives. What are the changing patterns and organisations of power and resistance that constituted the specific and changing definitions and self-definitions of women?

The changing patterns of life in a country working towards independence demanded a different reaction to what constituted a woman. She is no longer a stereotype. She changes accordingly and is capable of fluid identities. Yet she retains her Indianness. The women in *Prison and Chocolate Cake:* Tara, Rita and Lekha, Sarup Rani Nehru

(Vijayalakshmi Pandit, Sarojini Naidu (some true and some fictional) etc to name a few among the plethora of characters who inhabit the book are each in their own ways unique, not women whose reactions to situations are stereotypical from any perspective. They show none of the "weakness" commonly associated with women but what is remarkable is the fact that men in their relationships with women, do not treat them as such. It is a strong, healthy one based on mutual understanding and respect for their capabilities to be a part and parcel of the huge unfolding of history which was taking place.

Life as Nayantara sees it: Fiction, history and gender

The methodology here is not to go by individual books but by clubbing ideas which intersperse as useful for the core idea of this endeavour. The methodology is not linear time, it is cyclical.

The time in *This Time of Morning (1965)*is early post-independence time. The country is young and expectations high. Again, the society depicted is of high level politics. It was the time of Nehru as the P.M. "...a man of incorruptibility and vision, not only because of bonds forged long ago, but because this man had taken upon himself a challenge unique in history: that of raising a people to modern times with their own consent" (23)

Feminist historiography authenticates the identity and self of "woman" by placing her in a context and unless this context is elaborately studied and understood, the agenda of feminist historiography is not achieved. It is my firm belief that the character and identity of a woman emerges with the situation and Nayantara's women belong to this category. The demands of the situation are different and the perspective that goes with it changes. It is important to remember that it is situations and conflicts which mould men and women into right people and not inherent qualities. One is not born...is a tenet we cannot afford to forget.

This Time of Morning depicts the post independent years and with it is woven the myriad men and women characters who are inadvertently drawn into the flux of the moment. In a review of two novels by Nayantara Sahgal in 1970, Ruth Von Horn Zuckerman had said "India is changing with the times...(and they) **must** adjust their thinking to these changes". Further the novel had "long expository passages" and 'too many characters" and "Mrs Sahgal uses the omniscient point of view...but sometimes her leaping from the mind of the one character to another is confusing as are her time sequences in flashbacks." (emphasis mine) (84)[18]

India is not easy for the Western mind to comprehend. We live in cyclical time frame and hence our narrative pattern. And there is never a question of Indians "must adjust" situation in the novel. To understand Sahgal, it is essential to first situate her in a context and then read her characters, which is what this work attempts to do. We must leap with her as she moves from character to character and situation to situation.

---

[18] Mahfil Vol 6, No. 4 (Winter 1970) 84-87

Feminist historiography must grapple with these issues: the context, the narrative and the narrator and it is quite interesting to note that these boundaries blur when writing takes place because the connectivity in the mind is not compartmentalized. Instances cannot be segregated into separate spheres. The importance of a character is in the mind of the creator and the purpose with which he/she is created. Hence, if one were to look for precise marked boundaries, it would be a futile exercise. The analysis also shares this kind of crisscrossing of the boundaries.

The men in *This Time of Morning:* Rakesh, Kalyan Sinha, Sir Arjun Mitra, Saleem and others play an active part in the building of the nation. Sahgal reveals the ambitions, the desperation and the struggle of a nation in the making through these characters. The women: in relationship with these men or out are also important actors in the birth of a nation. Their relationship to each other and to the development of India as a nation and its ideologies come through subtly in the novel.

There are four relationships which are brought to the forefront. Saleem-Saira, Rakesh-Rashmi-Daleep- Neil, Uma –Arjun, Nita-Vijay-Kalyan. It is through these relationships perhaps that one can decipher the gendered structure of a particular time.

Rakesh, the Indian Foreign Service Officer (independent India's own contribution) returns to India after six years and finds a rapidly changing India.

Saleem Ahmed in charge of West Asia & North Africa "... a big untidy man..." greets Rakesh warmly. He realised that

"They all came back, himself included, from three, four, or five years abroad, sometimes much longer, and heaved a sigh of relief. But before a year was out they or their wives were agitating for foreign posts again." (3) Allowances were cut and accommodation was difficult and when everything was set about family, they were raring to go. Though they had come from orthodox conditions with arranged marriages, they had all acquired "polish and poise" (3) They were accustomed to "...the tempestuousness of Arab politics, the museums and art galleries of Europe, the impact of America. The wives "...spoke a smattering of several languages, and had babies and learned to keep house, servantless, all over the world. Even the most sheltered among them had obtained driving licenses', taken tennis lessons, learned to make cocktail and to entertain with ease. They did not really belong in Delhi or in any one place anymore." (3)

The tradition of feminist historiography has been one of reading between lines and through silences. The paragraph quoted above does not seem to have any gaps or silences. However, certain things emerge. There does not seem to be the presence of any sort of prejudices which we normally find in the Indian scenario of today. For instance, here man and woman are comfortable with variety, they move around the world with much gusto accepting change.

There is no rejection of the West, though there is this desire to return to India. It is not that only the men wanted to move, it was either "they or their wives" who wanted to move out. The women knew how to live their lives, even though they did not have a profession or even if they were not 'allowed' one. The list of activities that they indulged in meant a close access to the outside world, manners and customs and this is turn would have enriched each one of them. And there does not seem to be an opposition to this, coming in fact from Saleem, a Muslim! Contrary to the accepted beliefs of numerous people around the world of Muslims being conservative, Sahgal depicts a world where India was plural and plurality was acceptable. In fact people moved between pluralities with ease and comfort. In fact it would be surprising for the people of today to read Sahgal's Saira (Saleem's wife) hugging Rakesh warmly on his return, in front of her husband.(!!), which reminds us of stereotyping strategies in India.

We need to re- read ideologies of stereotypes created in India, either by the British or Indians themselves and make an endeavor to re- create the truths as one sees it and not as an aping of what was leftover by the Raj. Again this would mean an uphill task for feminist or gendered historiography because of the traditional mindsets of old school historians who would scoff at the idea of fiction being used for archival source! However the endeavor should persist.

Sir Arjun"... was at the top of the administrative tree, a patient, conscientious civil servant...(with)a quiet dignity and genuine sympathy for the young...his devotion to duty ...was a refuge from home and his wife" (8)

Neil Berensen, the architect of the Peace Institute describes Arjun's wife as "the woman with breasts – he could not describe her frank sensuality any other way" (27) Sir Arjun had considered "...Uma dead for many years" and sometimes wondered whether "had he been the corpse himself blocking his heart and mind and senses?"(28) Arjun's life was absorbed by work until a marriage was arranged for him. "He had been a dutiful son, a brilliant student and he filled his office with distinction" (31) until the arrival of Uma. "The smooth course of this idyllic existence was interrupted by the arrival of Uma – Uma who hated the dull districts after life in Calcutta. Uma in whom marriage had released a torrent of hungry sensuousness that brought to startling focus her exotic feline beauty'.(31) Arjun could not understand her boredom for he himself had never been bored. Her 'childlike petulance" that had so entranced him began to upset him. He could not understand why she could not occupy herself as all other women did. She was 'temperamental" and could fly into "rages", was "wild" and "lawless" and she was only twenty two! In marriage, they had drifted apart and lived as two separate people. She found solace in the arms of other men and when he began to believe the "disquieting" stories that circulated about her, he confronted her saying that she was putting their marriage in jeopardy.

"Uma's face had hardened as she flung back, "Marriage? What marriage?" It was then that he realized that she was an individual. She mocked him and told him all the unbelievable things in a way that left him "paralyzed with shock". (33) He retreated into work and a corner of his house. Work, however, did not suffer.

For a feminist reading, this episode in the life of Arjun and Uma would suffice to highlight the limited roles which women were forced to play and the ensuing desperation and hopelessness which came with it. What more could you expect from Uma, a young girl with only marriage as the goal? Or is it? In fact, there are no instances of a woman with a career in the novel. There are women who work but not as in a career. And even if they do, it always is in the position of subordination.

It is also important to note that virginity/chastity plays a crucial role in the life of a woman in India. However, a gendered reading could perhaps give us a peek into an entirely different world which would contribute in understanding the "Indian" mind and in the process discern the gendered relationship.

Sir Arjun's grandfather, Sarat Mitra, had been born at a time, when Bengal was coming into contact with the currents of European thought and he had been drawn like a magnet to the new English learning. When Lord Macaulay had launched English education in India, he had prophesied that it would"... spell the disappearance of Hinduism and herald the triumph of Christianity on the subcontinent." But Sahgal says that his optimism was as mistaken as that of a cavalcade of zealots before a succession of devout missionaries after him. For Hinduism was neither a creed nor a religion but a way of life sprung from the soil, the stones, the mountains and the rivers of India. The new learning came to India and with it the Bible's teaching. The Hindus received it. They honoured the gospel of Christ as they had that of the Buddha before him, and remained Hindus. (29)

Though Sarat Mitra was fascinated by the Bible, he did not embrace Christianity. He was impressed with its "singleness of purpose" and the "dynamic society" it brought into being and realised that religion was a snarl of taboos and abuses.

Education was the only way out. His grandson Arjun Mitra was sent to England when he was only fourteen and he returned for ICS examination. His marriage failed yet he knew that there was no escape from marriage. Hindu law had no provision for divorce. He lived with it and what sustained him was a passage from the Bible "Woman, where are those thine accusers? Hath no man condemned thee?... Neither do I condemn thee: go and sin no more.(35)

Instances such as these abound in the works of Sahgal. Christianity was viewed not as a threat but as one more way, albeit different, to view life. The characters of her novels are rooted in tradition, capable of seeing and knowing what was wrong. There does not seem to be a desire to move away but to move ahead, there was the need for reform, in their own beliefs and religious systems.

The conflict in the minds of the younger generations during the post independent era helps us to understand their struggle of coming to terms with a country which was complicated. It would be prudent to quote at length to bring to the forefront the "becoming" of the mindset of an India through Rakesh. He was

> ...puzzled over his chaotic heritage. Why could Hinduism not be easily defined? The Christian scriptures he had studied at school had clear, compelling commandments...It was a strong, serene, unambiguous religion. It had a holy book and Church, a heaven and a hell. So did Islam, and Islam, besides, overflowed the boundaries of religion to become a part of the daily life of Uttar

Pradesh, woven into its very earth and air. Music, poetry, and art, even the simple acts of speaking and eating would forever bear the stamp of Islam. Then why was Hinduism, the centre of consciousness, the creed he had been born into, the only baffling uncertainty? Why were there no commandments, no single scripture, no church to contain it? What were its beginnings, or did it have any, ancient as it was, beyond time, older then the rocks?

These misgivings of Rakesh are rhetorical as he himself explains

Hinduism was boundless enough...to encompass the loftiest of metaphysics, rigid enough to despise the Untouchable. It was goodness, and piety and the living light of faith, and Prayag...Allahabad's ancient name, was probably the only place in the world where kings had given all their riches in charity. Yet it was the sufferance of disease and clamor near the temple. It was a torpor that accepted maimed limbs, blind eyes and abject poverty as destiny, letting generations live and die in hopelessness, and at the same time it was the majesty of mind engaged in lifelong combat with the senses. You could not accept Hinduism in its entirety without harbouring ignorance and superstition too. You could not wholly reject it without destroying part of yourself, for it was the story of India... (India) was the great mosaic of peoples and tongues, faiths and philosophies, the sanctuary no seeker had ever been denied. It had been the home of Christian and

Jew since the first century, Muslim since the eighth. India did not simply tolerate religion. It nourished the very spirit of religion and in this it was very unique. (53)

And he concludes saying "...it was unique...it was ours..." (53)

So too Saleem. He chose India over Pakistan much to the consternation of his brother who had moved to Pakistan. But Saleem had thought of the assorted band of legislators who journeyed three times a year to Delhi and who had come from places which had not known a bus or an electric fan. The Lok Sabha for him "symbolized faith". For him it was the "custodian of the public conscience...the guarantee that no man could arise and say, 'I'm India'" (142)

This was the band of people who made and believed in India. These were men who had a purpose and who trusted in the institutions that India had created. There had been a common goal.

Historiography needs to grapple with the mind-set of the nation in the nascent stages. We need to go back in time and history to understand the conflicts and how they resolved it. We need to bring back those philosophical resolutions into today's troubled stage. In a way it is this "nourishment" which seeks to release people from a very narrow parochial attitude which is detrimental to development of not only the individual but also the nation.

The younger generation did not find the influences of the West as a threat either. Rakesh and Nita, representatives though of the elite, behave and enact a way of life common to the Westerners, easily. At 23(Rakesh) and 17 (Nita) life is full of infinite possibilities. They are not averse to partying, drinking and smoking, not that it means anything and for someone entrenched in traditional thinking, this would be taboo and of course the deduction that all this is a part of the western influence, yet at seventeen Nita has a firm head over her shoulders. At the talk of marriage, which as feminists would argue was the only available destiny or past time, Nita has some interesting things to say. She would like to marry "...someone with something interesting to say for himself..." but would not want somebody she can "Intimidate".(41) Along with Saira and Saleem, they share a easy camaraderie and Saleem is not averse to offering her a cigarette. Conversation flows easily with neither taking offence.

Rashmi, another character who is important and Rakesh's secret love, drops Berenson home after a party and is invited by him

> 'I don't know whether it is done or not, but I would like to ask you in for a drink'

> 'Well, you know there's a particular sort of prohibition here. There's a law to the effect that one can only have a drink in one's bedroom.'

> Neil laughed. "I do have a sitting room too'.

> 'It's a little late tonight,' said Rashmi (46)

This would not only be scandalous by traditional standards, but equally unacceptable. Yet the characters echo the times and no moral judgements are passed by the author. Women had a mind of their own and did not cry 'sexual harassment' at the drop of a hat. They were ready to take risks and were adventurous. For Nita "abroad" is magic.

To Rashmi, going through a broken relationship with her husband Dalip, Delhi provided a respite from the clashes that had become her relationship with him. It was a temporary relief from the deadening trauma out of which it seemed as though no feeling could ever again emerge. "I don't hate him," she had told herself wearily during the blank intervals between quarrels, "I don't wish him harm, but he and I – she could not think 'we' any longer – cannot go on together.... How like prolonged starvation wrong marriage could be, robbing lustre, defeating courage and will. (13)

Women take decisions and are willing to risk it rather than being bogged down by some mundane life order.

Rashmi – Neil Berensen's relationship constitutes an important part in the novel. Though, Neil is a foreigner they seem to be able to communicate. There is a free play of emotions. Neil's observation about the concept of happiness and marriage being two separate things is a view which Sahgal seems to endorse in her novels.

Rashmi's relationship with Neil restores her faith in the healing power of love and friendship. She is aware of her identity and therefore dissolves her marital ties. Rashmi thinks that relationships in marriage or outside can be made happy if the two sustain faith in each-other's integrity and uphold the value of love and harmony. Rashmi's divorce and her extra-marital relationship with Neil is the need for communication and emotional involvement of the self. Marriage makes Rashmi "...a moth trapped in cement." (12)

Rashmi's decision to separate from her husband comes as a mortal blow to all that her mother Mira had held sacred. "What reason under heaven could sever the marriage bond? Women stayed married, had since time immemorial stayed married, under every conceivable circumstance, to brutal insensitive husbands, to lunatics and lepers.... Fulfilment had lain in service and sacrifice. If there was suffering, too, it was part of life".(13) Sahgal is aware of the social conditioning of men and women which took place India. If Mira is aghast at Rashmi's decision, then Sir Arjun was no different either. Breaking out of the marriage was unthinkable. Marriage was still very much a community affair. Rashmi however does not belong to her generation.

Rashmi is not contented with the superficial acquaintance of Neil. She desires involvement and not the demanding relationship that exists in India between man and woman. Rashmi desires to explore Neil's life — the past, the present — its joy and despair but her desire is not comprehended by Neil. Space is a concept differently understood by the East and the West. In India, the private space is invaded, in the west, perhaps is free. Though there is, at the superficial level, an easy movement between the East and the West in turns of relationship, yet there are differences. Sahgal hints at the complexity of the relationship between Rashmi and Neil, which is turn becomes a metaphor for the complexity of the

Indian and his/her mindset which is caught in between two worlds colliding and co relating. It is through this relationship that she grows into an awareness of what she desires during her relationship with Neil. Their relationship also is a metaphor for the mindset of an Indian coming to grips with independence.

Relationships in Sahgal come in various dimensions. Some are happy and cherish the conventional values and others have a strong sense of individuality and an analytical mind, ready to break the imposed social and traditional walls to accept modern western values. In her novels, Sahgal reveals the changes in relations with women before and after marriage. In short, Nayantara Sahgal's women are of the view that they should move with the time and not compromise with the issue of their individual freedom in our male-dominated society. The feminist in Sahgal always insists on women's equality at par with men.

Uma and Leela, are women characters who play vital and modern multidimensional roles while establishing relations with others in both traditional and modern ways. These women search for freedom, using men as tools. Celia, Barbara and Nita, in their ultimate dependence on Kalyan perhaps are confused in their search for identity, but they take that much needed step.

What one needs to notice in such relationships is that Kalyan does not pass judgements on women and the roles they play. The women too do not press commitments from him.

In the character of Nita, Sahgal explores the father -daughter relationship. Nita is the young, beautiful daughter of Dr.

Narang, who is a queer blend of Eastern and Western culture. Western life-style is a part of Narang's culture but when it comes to his daughter, he would act in the most traditional manner, imposing severe restrictions on the movement of his ambitious daughter. Narang's family never allow their daughter to party. As Mrs. Narang puts it, "We don't allow Nita to go out alone. Her father would not hear of it." (4)

Narang's concern for the safety and protection of their daughter exemplifies their conformity to traditional values. Nita's parents would not allow their daughter to smoke, drink or attend dances till she is married. Modernity is at conflict with tradition. Family life and traditions echo the changing attitudes of the times and influences in society. This is a society caught in flux, a mindset emerging, not quite sure of how to tackle modernity. Interestingly nationalism through the family structure and traditions and culture had perhaps not yet begun. It would creep in later, in other forms of subtle control. It would creep in through movies, through the media, through politics, through a back-to-our-tradition and culture ideology much later. One has just to go through the timeline of movies produced in India to know how gradually and subtly the changes have taken place. I am reminded of one Bollywood movie, which became a runaway hit *Hum Aapke hai Kaun* [19], which was one of the first movies which impacted the audience to take a u turn away from westernization to 'authentic' Indian culture. The Indian film industry suddenly went ethnic and we took the complicated path to realizing ourselves as

---

[19] Bollywood movie, released on Aug 5th 1994 starring Salman Khan and Madhuri Dikshit, directed by Sooraj Barjatya

Indians. Many movies followed suit and pushed the country into more complicated grappling with nation, character and identity building.

Sahgal taps the confused and complicated identity of a generation which went through a different crisis in this novel. Nita's case is one such instance. Nita's discontent and the sense of uneasiness when she learns about her parent's decision to marry her off to a stranger is one such instance. Historiography has to grapple with this issue because home and sentiments connected with values are important in creating an identity and marriage is intimately connected with what the identity of what a person is and what he/she would become.

Finally, she agrees to her parents' choice of Vijay as groom only to lead an unsuccessful married life. Nita is fully aware that Vijay views her as a possession not as an individual, and this kind of marriage has no prospects of fulfillment. Nita desires to live her own life and discover the needs of her body, rejecting the values and ideas of the previous generation thrust upon her. In search of herself and freedom to get rid from the clutches of her husband, she rejects the so called anti-woman traditional values. She offers herself to the irresistible Kalyan, the man of her choice. She finds a strange comfort in his company and visits him frequently while decorating his drawing room. Once she directly refuses to go home and frankly expresses her love for Kalyan: "But don't make me go.....Don't make me go, please don't make me go." (6) He takes her to his room. Nita finds extra martial relationship with Kalyan more secure and comfortable, and necessary to fulfill her emotional hunger for life. When Kalyan asks her the reason for her frequent visits, she answers:

> I've thought about that so often.... Every time I came I wondered why. I used to think about it getting into the taxi and every minute the taxi took to come here, and all the while I was here. I didn't know why I came. I only knew I would die if I didn't.... Because I wanted to and it's the only thing I've ever really wanted to do". (7)

Nita's pre-marital relationship with Kalyan is the result of an attempt to fulfill her inner desire for love, emotional support and the need for communication. Sahgal's subjects are thinking subjects.

Interestingly, Sahgal's narrative "...never whines, even when the space ... is stifling. Instead, there is hope in the margins, where a character manifests as a human person with inherent dignity in whose presence stereotypes must shatter." (Joseph, Preface, x) Her characters are marginalized, but are symbols of human freedom and choice, they are agents rather than ideologically constructed subjects. And men play an important part in the creation of such subjects. At one end of the line, we have Sir Arjun, at the other there is Kalyan.

In a *A Time to be Happy* (1958), Maya is not comfortable with her husband and turns to social work and religion to fill in the vacuum. Sahgal is deeply concerned with the failure of marital relationships and the loneliness. Marriage is a bond which is repeatedly questioned and probed in her books. *Relationship,* a series of letters exchanged between Mangat

Rai and herself is a sensitive portrayal of relationships: both within and outside.[20] At this juncture, the temptation to quote a review about her book is irresistible. It begins

> This is the stuff that gossip writers dream of: famous, beautiful princess "happily married" to corporate tycoon falls wildly, madly, passionately in love with a bureaucratic Big Wheel, also "happily married"...

And asks

> But what, one finally wonders, is the point of publishing these thirty-year-old letters now? Sahgal offers a "feminist" justification: "How one woman reacted under stress, what she thought, felt, did, may interest other women..." [21]

The review is unsympathetic and a clear denial of the silences and the unseen punctuations in a woman's writing. He has missed it there but not in Mangat Rai, whom he says "...seeks to open larger questions".

The quotation is interesting

> Individuals must seek the transcendent ecstasies of love – a condition at once intensely narcissistic and passionately altruistic: "grace" to the secular, "socialism of the spirit" he calls it.

---

[20] Sahgal, Nayantara and E.N. Mangat Rai, *Relationships: Extracts from a Correspondence* Kali for Women 1994

[21] India Today June 30 1994

And then again

> There is sometimes destruction of the human fabric:
> It is a dilemma to which the low grade civil (and
> sometimes uncivil) war of bourgeoisie matrimony
> offers no solution[22]

> What brought in this detour is the need to point out
> the commonplace attitudes of the people who read
> this as "gossip" or as a tendency to fall in love. One
> does not have to read between lines, for the thought
> glares at you, the moment of truth stares at you,
> but is lost in the conditioned mindset about values
> inherent in the psyche. We not only refuse to see,
> we just cannot. A look at the letters, tell us about
> the "grace" and the "agony" of this relationship.
> There are commitments, there are values, and they
> must be upheld. There are things beyond "named
> relationships" and there are histories which cannot
> be named. Much before this book came out,
> Nayantara had tried to do it with her fiction.

Her characters experience loneliness and frustration. Maya
and her husband are unable to understand each other, which
result in lack of communication which in turn leads to
isolation in marriage. Maya is not ambitious. Hers is the
need for response and recognition of her existence in her own
house: "Not a good one or an approving one, necessarily,
just a response of any kind. Even when we live or die is not

---

[22] ibid

important unless it is important to someone."(1) Maya is a silent victim.

Maya and Ammaji suffer because they are unable to accept the relationships meekly. Ammaji and Maya are the representatives of the older generation and the transition period respectively. Sahgal shows her acute awareness of the dependent status of women on male in society. She is aware of the confining role of marriage as an institution for women. *A Time to be Happy* explores women's search for individuality both within marriage as equal partners and without it as individual. For Maya, marriage was doomed from the beginning, chiefly on account of the antithetical personalities of her husband and herself: "She had the cool purity of the eucalyptus, as compared with his extravagant gulmohur. She was the mirror-smooth lake to his rushing waterfall." (2)

Maya remains frustrated in her relations with her husband, and ultimately their marriage becomes sterile. The narrator's description of her as a slab of marble as 'marble in difference' is significant. What she considers the most important thing in life, is the emotional response which she is unable to receive from her husband. However, she receives it from the narrator. Maya is represented in contrast to the traditional ideal women. The narrator's mother supports her husband in all his views and enterprises. Like any true Hindu woman, she believes that "his concern was with God and hers with God in him." (3)

Lakshmi and Govind Narayan are the representatives of happy Hindu married couple. They are happy and always busy in domestic work and traditional rituals altogether. Both husband and wife are generous and sympathetic to each other and seem ready to sacrifice for other. In their smoothly run household one seldom heard the voices of the servants and the crying of the baby. Savitri, Kusum's mother, like a true Hindu woman, regularly observed fasts and offered prayers at five every morning for the well-being of her family generally and her husband particularly. The concentration on the traditional woman by Sahgal therefore serves to reveal the second vital function of Maya in the novel.

Ideology interpolates the woman as privileged to be the custodian of her husband and her children through her body or through the denial of her body. Since man is believed to be woman's superior through the mental, intellectual and spiritual sphere, she can become worthy of marital alliance only through moral uprightness, albeit sexual loyalty. In the Scriptures, it is the duty of the wife to ensure salvation for her husband via him. Hence the material benefit of a home and the spiritual benefit of death.

Women in the novel *Rich Like Us* reflect the experience entailed in being a part of highest rung of social hierarchy that has historically enjoyed access to wealth and political power.

While the variations fracture notions of a monolithic Indian woman, at yet another level they also highlight workings, of what Rajeshwari Sunder Rajan elaborates as, the double and contradictory sense of the idea of "belonging to" their class, caste etc as this belonging can result in both privilege and oppression. Therefore ""belonging to" has a double and contradictory sense as it means both "affiliated to" and "owned by": the one indicating voluntary and participatory membership, the other secondariness, functionalism and (merely) symbolic status"(Rajan 4).

Sahgal's women react to the condition of "secondariness" and attempt to explore, transform and challenge insufficient and limiting versions of roles such as that of a mother, wife or a daughter mandated to them within the dominant definitions and ideologies of family and society. "... differences in religion, caste, class and rural/ urban setting pose a challenge for a "viable feminist politics", "in the interest of a transformative politics, differences must be managed, if not transcended" (Rajan 3).

Differences in religion, caste, class and rural/ urban setting produce variations in the practices of patriarchy that produce variations in the experience of being a mother and a wife. For example, the women's work in the household that consists of series of tasks that need to be done each day is singularly a woman's responsibility in these novels. Her absence even for a day is "serious for the household" as no one would do her work in her absence (Krishnaraj 37). The is due to the assumption that traits such as self-denial, nurturing, care-giving etc are intrinsic to women be it even the elite Kashmiri Brahmin housewives in *Rich Like Us*

In *Rich Like Us,* Sonali's mother, who belongs to elite society, begins her daily routine at 4 a.m with fetch water from the well followed by housework, grinding spices and the rest. Even when she is physically indisposed after one of her many pregnancies, she would cook by "leaning out of bed to stir dal on the stove" (30). The comparison makes apparent that due to essentialist notions of women as self denying nurturers and caregivers, the household duties are sole responsibility of the women. However due to the different social locations, the characters make use of different mechanisms to cope with the pressure to do so.

A problematic relation between the mother and daughter is depicted in *Rich Like Us*. Sonali's moral and intellectual development is fostered by her highly educated father who for instance is described as having inducted her into Gandhian values. On the contrary her mother is unable to transcend regressive caste based discourses and is heard complaining that after independence "untouchables [were] behaving like everyone else" (188). In the novel when the Emergency is declared, Sonali is with her father and has unspoken access to his thoughts- a connection that the text falls silent about with regards to her mother. "Papa was thinking of battles for freedom fought and won and all that sacrifice now come to this" (198). Such an analysis seems to suggest a juxtaposition of the father – mother image where the image of mother is devalued because of the assumption of inability to transcend traditional discourses and engage with the new project of nation building.

Significantly each of her novels includes women who reject the roles of stereotypes along with the very institution of marriage Sonali in *Rich Like Us*. These women challenge the idea of "motherhood as the primary destiny of women" and hence refuse to be confined to the domestic tasks of mothering, feeding, nurturing and caring for the members of the household (Krishnaraj 36). In choosing to do so they risk being devalued, discredited and deemed as superfluous by their families and society.

All these novels highlight the role of education which makes gainful employment possible. Gainful employment in turn enables resisting various forms of marginalization. The idea that the wife needs to possess lower caliber than the husband is a common hurdle to their education. Sonali tops the civil services exam, but finds that her abilities threaten men such as Kachru. Even though none of these novels depict a denouement where the heroine acquires a definitive knowledge of her true self, the heroines embrace the future with hope and confidence which their education enables. Sonali observes that she "was young and alive, with… century stretched out before… waiting to be lived" (301).

Change and Nayantara Sahgal

It is interesting to see how Nayantara Sahgal's women characters respond to the phenomenon of change. The India she depicts is one filled with volatile changes in society and temperaments. How do these women cope with the opposing pulls of tradition, taboos, conditioning, modernity etc in their quest for independence and identity? How do they find meaning in life? How does the changing India chart out their path to self-fulfillment and the creation of a selfhood? Does it help or does it create more difficulties?

Sahgal cannot be read in a vacuum. She has to be a part of the long line of writers who have tried in different ways to discuss the India that they have seen, albeit from different perspectives. They have reacted to these questions of tradition, modernity etc in different ways. And each of these writers have something relevant to say because they have been participants of this ever changing concept called India.

The work of Mulk Raj Anand, R. K. Narayan, Raja Rao, and a host of other novelists is meaningful, to me, as part of this ongoing and evolving "big" story. Simply, we are all a part of one big story or protonarrative, our own "little" stories adding to its totality. We are not only a part of it, but also, in our own ways, making it happen, altering it in trying to understand and define it, in relation to ourselves. This big story is the story of the growth and development of modern India, starting at the beginning of the nineteenth century and continuing down to the present day. (Paranjape 20)

These issues could be examined in certain novels of Sahgal. *This Time of Morning* (1966), *Storm in Chandigarh* (1969), *The Day in Shadow* (1971), *A Situation in New Delhi* (1977), and *Rich Like Us* (1985) could be the site of focus.

All the novels are women centered. Bad marriages make some of them walk out while others try to grapple with the problem of single women and their attempt to survive in this patriarchal world. They tend to grapple with the problem of trying to find ways and means of surviving in this male dominated society because of either being too traditional or moderately modern, which brings us to the issue of tradition and modernity. How do the creations of Sahgal confront this problem of tradition versus modernity? In fact what does tradition and modernity mean in India? How do we understand it? To the West we are a traditional, sometimes conservative society. Within India, we have conflicting standards. The vastness of India is itself a challenge. The country is so large and so varied that to say we are either traditional or modern could be a misnomer. If geography is one challenge, then situations could be another. If one looks at the varied cultures, practices and belief systems operating in this country, then one is dazzled by its sheer canvas of conflict between what is traditional and what is modernity. And then there is the question of caste, class, region etc the list goes on.

To Paranjape "... tradition and modernity (are not) automatically opposed to each other. He says that

> ... there is the potential for modernity and change in tradition. Likewise, I see tradition as not necessarily evil. If by tradition is meant all that is handed down to us, then certainly not all of it can be bad. Tradition, then, is the repository of both good and evil, and its use and abuse must be separated from tradition itself. Similarly, modernity cannot be all good if it simply denotes the latest. Not everything in the present or from recent times can be of positive value; much of it, in fact, is more horrible both qualitatively and quantitatively than anything humankind has witnessed in the past. Both tradition and modernity are mixed categories, descriptive rather than normative. Because they are value-loaded, we cannot see them in simple unitary terms. We must be alive to their inner contradictions, tensions, and oppositions and be aware of their overlaps and interpenetrations. (1994,3)

Sahgal's characters operate in an elite society and the standards of tradition / modernity has already shifted in the minds of readers on what is expected of them. In the book on Sahgal (1976), A. V. Krishna Rao addresses himself to this question of tradition and modernity:

> Unlike some other Indian novelists in English who indiscriminately affirm the Indian cultural milieu, she seeks to excoriate the diseased and the decadent part of the Indian tradition. She does not however go with Mulkraj [sic] Anand in making loud and strident protests against the concept of conformity to tradition in favour of some alien idea of social justice; on the contrary, she dives deep into the sustaining springs of the composite cultural tradition of India and comes up to affirm that aspect of Indian tradition which possesses and promises a survival value. She is thus neither an out-and-out conformist nor a thoroughbred nonconformist. She is neither too submissive to the dictates of an orthodox tradition nor too much in love with revolutionary romanticism. She accepts the composite character of the Indian tradition and affirms its catholicity which allows for the human being maximum freedom.(4)

Rao finds that Sahgal takes the middle path between tradition and modernity. Unlike Raja Rao, who emerges as a traditionalist, or Anand, who is mostly anti tradition, Sahgal is somewhere in the middle. But he does not evaluate the content of her work. However he has sketched for us the framework and we have to traverse the path.

Jasbir Jain speaking about Sahgal says," There is much in tradition which she values and a great deal in modernity which she rejects,"(5) Paranjape feels that she fails to point out exactly what Sahgal values in tradition and what she rejects in modernity. In this context it is interesting to note that the question of tradition-modernity and the position of women in India is supplied by Sahgal herself. In several interviews she has stated that one of her major themes is the definition of the virtuous woman: "Right from the beginning my women have been a sort of new definition of the virtuous woman. The virtuous woman, according to tradition, is ideally a kind of 'sati', i.e. one whose life ends in self-immolation. She is there to suffer, to stay put, and to endure all the problems that come her way. My women, right from the start of my novels, have walked out."(6) The same idea is repeated in Sahgal's "Meet the Author" address organized by the Sahitya Akademi in 1988.

In Sahgal's works the women move away from the stereotype of the virtuous woman ushering in a new definition of virtue. They walk out of marriage. This in itself is a momentous decision. It very clearly says that they do not accept "virtue" as handed down to them and though they still do not have a clear idea of what is it that they want, they nevertheless are ready to take the jump. Rashmi, Saroj and Simrit walk out, defying 'Sati' and the concept of "virtue" endorsed by it. They are determined to live with courage and self respect. Her virtue is courage, which is a willingness to risk the unknown and to face the consequences [23].These words echo, almost exactly, what Saroj says to Vishal in *Storm in Chandigarh*. When Vishal asks her, "And have you known

---

[23] Nayantara Sahgal, "Passion for India," Indian Literature, 1988, p. 84

ambition?" she replies: "I want to be a virtuous woman" (SC, 230).

All these quotations emphasize Sahgal's commitment to change. She places woman at the heart of the tradition-modernity issue; she becomes the site where the battle between the two is fought. It is clear that as far as the status of women is concerned, Sahgal is completely against what she perceives to be tradition. In "Passion for India" she points out that the background for the personal crisis in her novels is usually political: "And alongside the personal story there is a picture of political erosion, degradation and decay" (PI, 85).

Sahgal's Feminist Priorities *Rich Like Us:*

Sahgal is looked up to as one of the main feminist writers in India, and she has admitted her preference for focalising politics through the experience of living as "a woman", through the construction of women characters in interaction with the private and political dimensions of varied systems of power.[24]

Sahgal's represents Indian society through her women characters as well as the men characters. Her representation takes for granted the active role educated women are expected to play in politics, business, management and economy.

---

[24] This is the gist of Sahgal's presentation in the Encycolpaedia of Post colonial Literatures in English, Benson and L.W.Conolly (eds) Routledge, London and New York, 1994, Vol I and II

However, she equates the possibility of women's professional participation in any sector of activity, and the corresponding possibility of liberation, with the accompanying development of a socialist project for postcolonial India. Due to this, she is able to link the historical processes set in motion with the transition to an independent India to a deep social transformation, which would naturally affect women's condition. Indian postcoloniality thus amounts to an open project, where new roles for women should evolve together with a more general change in Indian mentalities. It is in this sense that one of the main characters, Sonali, remembers her father's vow of confidence on the dawn of independence: "Women like you, are going to Indianise India" (Rich Like Us 28). In this context, it meant that the recreation of an independent Indian identity, free from British colonialism would be created. It also meant that educated trained women were expected to play an important role in the reconstruction of India's renewed identity and more importantly it would not be contained within the domestic sphere.

The confluence of colonialism and female oppression makes the formulation of the project of postcolonial future the ground for the liberation of women. However this might run the risk of presenting the postcolonial independence as a process of loss of tradition which has always been interpreted as loss of cultural identity, given the importance of nationalist mentalities then. Under the conservative sectors and mind-set of the society then, nationalism must have been a highly sensitive subject in postcolonial India, as part of the consolidation of its post-independence identity, especially since the nation was already reeling under the problem of Partition and Sikh secession. In such a scenario, how would one go about defending reform and women who were critical of India's traditions, without looking like anti nationals?

Sahgal is careful here. She specifies through her two women characters, Sonali and Rose that she defends an adapted kind of socialism, integrated with India's ways. She negotiates India's role models within the framework of political organisation. The link to the postcolonial context of India is made via the fact that historical changes imply transition moments, and these tend to be prone environment to try reforms. Within the frame of Sahgal's arguments, the contradiction between changing sexist traditions and the assertion of India's cultural identity would be settled by socialism because this ideology expects from women a modern, active participation in society, meaning the' socialist nation' would automatically settle women's issues.

The postcolonial India depicted in *Rich Like Us* in India is different. It was Emergency and a time of traditional mentalities. This perhaps explains why India's fragmented social landscape will probably remain unchanged among high caste communities, like the Kashmiri Brahmins. The link between caste and power, caste being inherited by birth for males and by marriage for women, explains the strength of gendered codes.

Sonali is an interesting character in *Rich Like Us*. She is unorthodox and it through her unorthodoxy that the direction of the post-independence change regarding traditional feminine identities in India can be seen. She is a Western educated, high caste woman, who used to be the Joint Secretary of the Ministry of Industry. Her serious commitment to socialism has prevented her from sensing the change in the political atmosphere around her and only when she is dismissed, on grounds which are not very clear, does she realise that she is out of tune with the new political priorities for those in power. Her life and career is presented in contrast with marriage, the two options for women with marriage being high on the priority and respect list. Sonali chooses career and the moment of epiphany is the marriage of her friend Bimmie. Sahgal colourfully describes the scene.

> Kiran and I followed her into the room where the bride waited, looking like a tent. I couldn't see her face under the crimson and gold sari pulled so low over her forehead. But I was hypnotised by Bimmie's nose ring, the sandal paste dots on her face, eyes downcast, and those manacled hands resting submissively in her red silk lap.

> This was never Bimmie. "Hey Bimmie!" I hissed. She looked up and it was her in the tent and the chains and the dots, nobody else. Wails welled up in me, erupting like claps of thunder into the room. "You'll get a good thrashing when I get you home, Sonali, I don't know what's come over you."

> …Your turn will come, little darling, never worry"..

> …busybodies fussed around Bimmie, tilting her head, fiddling with bangles and chains, stroking her cheek, praising her sweet docile nature, which

> made it clear they knew nothing about Bimmie
> and had captured and tented her by mistake. My
> wailing protest did nothing to keep Bimmie's future
> at bay. (54)

Sahgal's picturisation is brilliant. Bimmie is portrayed as docile, passive and submissive. She is objectified as a 'tent" and expected to be the stereotype of a bride and the acceptable woman. Sonali no longer recognises her friend in the comments of other people around her and Sahgal suggests the annihilation of the bride's identity. She is no longer an individual, but a stereotype, of a bride who is chained, captured and manacled. Interestingly Sonali's tears are mistaken to be a cry to be part of this ornate charade. Here is a stereotype of bride and Sonali's hysterical reaction to this is what prompts her refusal to conform. Sonali is driven to 'frantic competition, to stardom in…studies, to deliverance from suitable 'boys' and 'marriage abroad'(57)

For Sonali this is not an easy decision for, choosing a career over marriage in the Indian context is still not acceptable. Ironically people who do look down upon such women are still capable of 'accepting' them if they have power and financial stability. Within the novel, Sahgal presents for us the other side of the divide. There are other women characters who have 'opted' for marriage. Kiran, Sonali's sister is not much concerned with what has happened to Sonali as long as relations with the 'top" are in good measure. In Kiran's head, the world is the size of her caste and family, and 'power makes for diety", which means that mature, critical socio-political awareness is replaced by allegiance. She cannot understand Sonali's professional pride and her ethical disappointment with the system. Kiran's world is domestic, it stays that way.

Sonali's trials do not end here. Time and again, she is made to conform. Recovering from hepatitis and also dismissal, and intending to comfort her, her doctor praises her resistance and endurance, as the qualities that enable women to survive within the frame of their female condition. Being a woman, though ill and cut off from a brilliant career, Sonali is comparatively well off and she should be pleased with her luck.

> When I was a child, I remember my mother getting up at 4 am to walk with the other women to the well to fetch water. Then she got down to the housework, grinding spices and the rest. She had seven children, unassisted. Three of them died before they were a year old. I remember her after one of her pregnancies, leaning out of bed to stir the dal on the stove. The kind of life that makes for courage (34)

Sonali has no stomach for this. She knows that she has suffered and does not believe that it is just. Nor does she agree with the idea that this gives her endurance and therefore can be termed courageous. She does not believe that women should be entitled to less but have to bear more hardships. By creating a character like Sonali, who is very modern and critical towards established views concerning women, and also high caste Kashmiri Brahmins, Sahgal is suggesting new patterns of feminine identity more attuned to professionalism, alternate identity other than that of the role models of sister, daughter, mother etc towards that of social responsibility. She fights against notions of 'marriage and stability' which for her are imprisonment and lead to annihilation. These, she believes makes women 'inanimate objects' within the frame of caste codes and family hierarchies.

It seems fairly clear that, in novel after novel, Sahgal expresses her dissatisfaction with the "new" in politics. The new, the modern, is often corrupt, ruthless, and fascistic. The old, the traditional, is the Gandhian, the humanistic, and the compassionate, which the modern displaces.

To sum up, critics have recognized that Sahgal works out a kind of synthesis between tradition and modernity. She accepts some aspects of the former and rejects others; likewise, she accepts some aspects of the latter and rejects others. But what she rejects and accepts is not clearly indicated, either by the critics or by Sahgal. The author, however, does tell us quite emphatically that she sees tradition as being the main cause for the enslavement of women. Her women rebel against such traditions, which would force them to suffer silently, without redress. Instead, her women walk out, substituting courage for self-sacrifice, thereby redefining the notion of the virtuous woman.

In Sahgal's novels one sees tradition acting in two ways. One is in religion and the other in politics. Religion is important here because this is what determines what a person does or how they behave in India. Women carry cultural baggage's in their lives, hence it is pertinent that religion is a factor to be reckoned with They are moral upholders of tradition and all that is 'good' in religion. The belief systems of Hinduism are therefore the guidelines for women on how to behave and act.

Paranjape sees that this tradition in politics is also responsible for political attitudes, for how a particular culture responds to corruption and the abuse of power. However, in Sahgal's world, politics is an area in which we Indians have our own positive tradition because of the national struggle for independence. This tradition, chiefly, is the combined legacy of Mahatma Gandhi and Jawaharlal Nehru. There is in it the Gandhian emphasis on truth, nonviolence, satyagraha, social justice, prayer, poverty, simplicity, and so on, and the Nehruvian emphasis on socialism, democracy, and progress. In addition, there is a third realm on which the question of tradition and modernity has bearing. This has to do with the values and life-choices of the main characters, especially as they are revealed in intimate relationships. It is necessary to examine how these three kinds of tradition are depicted in Sahgal's novels. Only then can we form some idea of her own brand of synthesis between tradition and modernity. (Ibid)

Hinduism seems to be a determining factor in her novels. In "Passion for India" she admits that Hinduism is one of the important themes in her novels.

> What does it [Hinduism] mean today? How does this culture affect our conduct, our decisions, that sort of thing? What kind of person is the inheritor of this inheritance? Hinduism is of interest to me because most of us are Hindus, but even those

who aren't, live under the social and psychological overhang of Hinduism. It is not something we can ignore, if we want to understand ourselves. (PI, 85)

It is clear that Sahgal believes that the way we behave or rather the choices that society gives us have to do with this system of beliefs and practices called Hinduism. This is obvious when we take a closer look at her characters, especially the women. Once Rashmi's marriage begins to disintegrate, she is forced to ask herself what system it is which expects her to suffer and suffer silently without reacting or trying to change her life. Significantly, Hinduism becomes an issue only in *This Time of Morning* (1966). *A Time to Be Happy* (1958), her first novel, shows no concern or conflict with the prevailing ideology of Hinduism. The conflict arises only when Rashmi, in the next novel, contemplates separation from Dalip. Hinduism, it would seem, is all right as long as one does not break any of its implicit codes. When one does, then one is forced to confront its hypocrisies, double standards, and oppressions. Only those who are burned, so to speak, by the system are forced to question it. They can no longer accept all that is perpetrated in the name of tradition.

It is Kailas in *This Time of Morning* who first addresses this issue in Sahgal's fiction, and Kailas seems to function as the author's spokesman in this case, because he is invested with enormous narrative approval and authority. Not only is he a positive character who enjoys much authorial power, but his view of Hinduism is repeated, with slight modifications, by other characters like Vishal, Raj, and Sonali's father Keshav. Hinduism, for Rakesh, is a puzzle because it seems so chaotic; "the creed that he was born into" was "the only baffling uncertainty" (*This Time of Morning*, 40). To help him, Kailas explains:

> Hinduism was boundless enough . . . to encompass the loftiest of metaphysics, rigid enough to despise the Untouchable. It was goodness and piety and the living light of faith. . . . Yet it was the sufferance of disease and clamor near the temple. It was torpor that accepted maimed limbs, blind eyes and abject poverty as destiny, letting generations live and die in hopelessness, and at the same time it was the majesty of the mind engaged in lifelong combat with the senses.

The picture of Hinduism painted by Kailas underscores Sahgal's ambivalence toward it. This ambivalence is summed up by the narrator: "You could not accept Hinduism in its entirety without harbouring ignorance and superstition too. You could not wholly reject it without destroying part of yourself, for it was the story of India." (ibid) Essentially, this is Sahgal's view of tradition through all her work.

Rashmi, Saroj, Simrit, Mona, and Rose, Sahgal's heroines, all suffer the brunt of the negative aspects of Hinduism. The prototype of the woman oppressed by marriage begins with Rashmi. When she decides to walk out on her husband, her mother Mira is unhappy: "Rashmi's announcement was worse than bad news. It was a mortal blow to all she held sacred. . . . What reason under heaven could sever the marriage bond? Women stayed married, had since time immemorial stayed married, under every conceivable circumstance, to brutal insensitive husbands, to lunatics and lepers" (*This Time of Morning*, 146). The last words would seem to echo Manusmriti itself, wherein a woman is enjoined to remain true and faithful to her husband regardless of the latter's character or treatment of her.(8) (Manu does allow a woman to leave her husband if he is insane (9:79), but he enjoins fidelity upon a wife whose husband is unfaithful (5:154 and 9:80); the husband, of course, can leave an unfaithful wife (9:80).

This is an example of how conventional Hinduism oppresses a woman. It must be admitted, though, that we never get to know exactly what went wrong between Rashmi and Dalip. Also, Mira's views do not seem to be true to her character, because her own marriage to Kailas was so unconventional. Here she comes across as a very conservative person, whereas the father, Kailas, is more understanding.

Saroj and Simrit are clearly victims of patriarchal oppression. In both their marriages there is a clash of values leading to incompatibility. I shall focus later on the values involved, but it is sufficient to note how in both these marriages the women are not only considered automatically subservient by their husbands, but the final break comes because of the violation of the unstated rule of obedience which the husbands think their wives must follow. In both marriages the woman is little more than slave or property. Inder's fixation on Saroj's one-time sexual experience during her student days becomes an insurmountable barrier in their relationship. Inder's ideas about his wife's supposed violation of chastity before her marriage are not so much irrational as tribal; though educated, he thinks of her unconsciously as a fallen woman, soiled or secondhand goods, so to say. His wife-battering too comes from the same possessive instinct. Lalli, Som's friend in *The Day in Shadow*, had killed his wife for being unfaithful; Som "kills" Simrit financially through a very unfair divorce settlement. Similarly, Ram, though already married to Mona, marries Rose and goes on to have an affair with Marcella, all with a frightening nonchalance which would imply that he considers it his right to behave this way. Therefore, all these women are oppressed by tradition. The patriarchal version of Hinduism tolerates the oppression of women by men.

This version of Hinduism reaches its height in *Rich Like Us*, where we see an upper-class/caste woman of an educated, "progressive" family being forced to commit sati in 1905. This is Sonali's great-grandmother. No wonder that the strongest indictment of Hinduism is found in this novel. Outraged over his mother's murder/self-immolation, unable to find any way of explaining it to himself, Keshav's grandfather writes: "So I cannot believe in Hinduism, whatever Hinduism might be. Not because of such evils as sati, but because evil is not explained" (136). In addition, we are told of the rape and killing of lower-caste/class women. This happens routinely in Uttar Pradesh and Bihar and ironically it happens everywhere in modern India today. Sahgal mentions the names of several cities and towns where women are fed to brick kilns after they have been abused-- "Muzzafarpur, Samastipur, Bhojpur, Beguserai, Monghyr, Purnea, Gaya, Patna, Chapra" (68). Finally, Rose herself is murdered by her stepson Dev. All these, then, are instances of the oppression of women by tradition.

The conflict between tradition and modernity is brought to us in yet another way by Sahgal. If religion and politics are two ways, then the oppression of women through caste, primarily the Kashmiri Brahmin is something that Sahgal discusses in the novel *Rich Like Us*. How religion is an oppressive factor in the life of women is repeatedly brought to us by Sahgal. Closely connected to this is the oppression of women though the aspect of caste. "We are Kashmiris, and Kashmiriness is the more powerful for inhabiting a territory of the imagination" (55) Collective identity in India of a particular caste is carefully built up. A caste is known by its distinctive behaviour which could or could not be disciplined by ritual (if there is one) and is inculcated from childhood with a set of beliefs and values which marks its boundary from the 'other'. Interestingly Kashmiriness is acquired by birth/or marriage. Marriages in India usually are contracts and in lineage, are political contracts on which rests the future of the community. It is a medieval system in which women are exchanged through the males of an allied group as a means to strengthen collective identity.

Through Rose, a character in *Rich Like Us* Sahgal discusses the problems that high caste women face. Rose is the barren, British wife of Ram and shares him with his first wife, Mona and lover Marcella. She is insecure given the Hindu household and the inability to conceive (which in itself is a grave misfortune in the Indian context). However she is accepted and sometimes respected too but the problem arises when Ram has had a stroke, is in a coma and Rose has to live with her step son and his wife Nishi. Rose's position is that of the wife-widow-mother-in-law position, something which is so alien to her as she is the other. When Ram dies, the question of sharing property arises. There is clearly no intention to give a share to Rose, because her presence was always resented.. It is here that one gets a glimpse into what constitutes the plight of a widow according to the Hindu Succession Act.

In 1956 the Hindu Succession Act granted female children equal claims with male children to inherit property. In 1957, the Hindu Code Bill established the rights of a widow over inherited property, on an equal basis with other relatives. However, one must remember that laws are one and execution is quite another matter. Sonali's memories are testimonies to what actually happens to widows in the Indian context. She mentions the 'shaven headed little girls wrapped in grimy saris" who "waited for leftover food to be thrown to them from the saint's kitchen, Child widows. Their karma. Nothing to be done" (56)

Rose is aware of her plight and approaches Sonali for help. Surprisingly no lawyer dares to fight Devikins because of his proximity to Indira Gandhi. Everybody tells her that since Dev "is doing splendidly", it would be better if she came to an understanding" (93) with her step son. Even though Sonali insists on a legal arrangement, nobody wants to "upset" him. Deftly, citing family convenience, and private issues, the legal procedures are always cancelled and the woman is always the oppressed one. One is aware of not only marginalization of woman, but also the fact that the domestic arena is not something which protects all the time. In fact, under the sanction of the "family" the woman suffers oppression and the law is ineffective in dealing with it. As though to drive home this point, Rose is murdered at the hands of her stepson's men. And conveniently, as always, her death is an accident: she fell in the well and drowned. This brings down the curtains completely.

Mona is also a victim of this kind of social situation. Her suicide is termed as an accident, the oil lamp of the prayer table fell, and her sari caught fire. But fortunately she is saved by Rose and a new bonding develops between Mona and Rose. Very subtly Sahgal reveals to us the other side of women's relationships, thereby unsettling another of many misconceived misconceptions of relationships between women. Man is not a contention here, identity is. For Mona and Rose, the identity of being women and handling a crisis together is important. This was not done because they share something in common, Ram but that the plight of women is precarious within the family and they rely on this understanding and gain courage. Sahgal however, makes the readers reflect on "accidents" which happen randomly in India.

The issue of Sati is also discussed by Sahgal. For Sahgal, sati is murder and claims a huge dimension of national guilt and self-awareness from the people on the continent. She feels that one has to confront the past in modern times to realise the issue of violence against women. In fact the chapter on Sati goes back to 1829, the year that sati was legally abolished by the British through a manuscript written by Sonali's grandfather, in 1915 and interestingly this manuscript is produced as evidence of the willingness of few citizens who were against this practice. Sahgal denies that sati was committed with the widow's consent, most of the time they were drugged or sedated and hence the absence of screams or protests of any kind. Secondly, she tells us that some of them have tried to run away. All this information is brought to the readers as pieces of news. She narrates how the relatives of a Brahmin widow twice grab her and throw her back to the fire, beating the sense out of her with logs from the pyre. Sahgal, also tells us about the power of superstition and social pressure in the act of sati.

At yet another level, Sati becomes an instrument for politics and manipulation of votes. Saints and religious speakers emerge out of nowhere, preaching a return to fundamentalism and one knows the agenda behind this. It is quite interesting to see that what happened then is happening now, in the political sphere, though perhaps the tools are different. The agenda seems to be the same. Perhaps there is this insecurity of identity which haunts people. There seems to be some fear of being overpowered by forces which you do not understand. And man, in his ignorance, allows powers of some other kind to overpower them, not really comprehending that it is bringing in the same kind of chaos. Religion has this ability within it, for belief in religion is faith and faith has never been rational. How else in India, does one explain the practice of Sati then and honour killings now? Why does the woman's body always be the site of violence?

That act of Sati has other dimensions as well. In the novel, Sonali's grandfather dies. Relatives, unknown, until then arrive, and because the child is underage, an uncle claims the inheritance of the house and family assets. The widow and her son take refuge in law to protect the son's interests. However, the son is witness to his mother "burning" when he returns home from college and is told that she accepted Sati. The son (Sonali's grandfather) is sent to England to study. Sonali later tells us that the spot later became a pilgrimage site where the last woman on the region committed Sati. (252)[25] In fact, if newspapers are to be believed, then the problem of sati still persists in our country.[26]

As seen and experienced in other parts of India and as history has to tell us, communal identity breeds intolerance towards others.

If women are treated badly by tradition, what about men? The answer will depend on what our own values are. From one standpoint, Dalip (of whom we know little), Inder, Som, and Ram are triumphant. They dominate their women and seem to win, at least materially. But surely, these men are very unhappy; in fact, they ultimately end up losers. Their marriages break up, and worst of all, their lives are completely devoid of love. They have internalized the violence of the patriarchy and in turn directed it outward at their wives. They have been handed down expectations about "husbandhood" and "wifehood" which are incompatible with contemporary reality. In brief, tradition has turned them into oppressors. Their tragedy is that they are incapable of introspection or change and must be abandoned by their spouses in the end.

---

[25] The spot of pilgrimage reminds us of Roopkanwar who committed Sati in the district of Shekhavathi in September 1987 -

[26] According to the Chicago Tribune, another Sati was committed on Nov 11, 1999 by Charan Shah a dalit. Nov 18 1999. Another occurred in August 2002 in Madhya Pradesh, when Kuttubai died on her husband's pyre. She was 65 years old. (Indian Express Bureau, 6th Aug, 2002, Internet network news.)

There is another type of man, though, in Sahgal's novels. Sanad, Rakesh, Vishal, Raj, Osman, and, to some extent, Ravi Kachru are representatives of this type. All these men are liberal, compassionate, and seek more or less equal relationships with women. What distinguishes them is the fact that they do not aspire to dominate over women. These men, however, are almost always critical of tradition--or, rather, they embody another kind of tradition. They are, critics of the establishment. Usually they are Gandhians.

Often they allow the beleaguered woman to escape the tyranny to which she has been subjected. One reason *Rich Like Us* is so depressing is the fact that such a man is absent; there is no way out for Rose.

Hence, we have seen that the effect of tradition on Sahgal's women is, by large, inimical. Women who are quite placid, passive, and conformist are forced by circumstances to rebel. Their oppression is so great that they have no choice. In Sahgal's novels divorce becomes a powerful symbol of revolt against tradition. The assertion of freedom by the women indicates their refusal to accept patriarchal gender relations. This freedom--which critics have pointed to repeatedly as a prime value in her work--to act, create, and live the way a woman wants to includes sexual freedom. From *This Time of Morning* onward, the heroines decide whom to make love to without being afraid of social consequences. Rashmi sleeps with Neil, a pattern repeated in Devi's affair with Michael in *A Situation in New Delhi*. Saroj and Skinny have had sexual encounters with their peers while still at college. Sonali and Kachru have been lovers at Oxford. The Sahgal heroine's attitude toward herself is not influenced by conventional notions of purity/contamination. This is best summed up in Saroj's comments about herself to Vishal: "I've always loved myself. . . . I've been able to say I mattered, that I was whole and clean. But today, for the first time, someone else has said it. It's like seeing a rainbow" (SC, 198). In this passage we see once again a redefinition of virtue. It lies not necessarily in sexual purity, but in the kind of values one has.

Rashmi, Saroj, and Simrit, in choosing personal happiness over suffering, affirm certain modern, post-Renaissance notions about self-fulfillment. They value the individual over the collective; they value personal fulfillment over social obligation. Moreover, their actions assume a certain idea of individuality which tradition would seem to deny them. They seek freedom to act, to change, to combine, and to create--options not available to them within a conventional marriage. Tradition would appear to force men and women to stick to their given roles, discharging well-defined duties. In opposing their assigned roles, the women are choosing modernity over tradition. As Vishal tells Saroj, "It has taken a million years of evolution for a person and his cherished individuality to matter . . . and no terror must be allowed to destroy that" (SC, 231). Life with Inder would have amounted to accepting not just a loss of individuality, but, by extension, a kind of living death.

The right to choose, once again, underscores the value of freedom in Sahgal's work. Krishna Rao was the first to recognize that freedom for Sahgal was a cardinal value, an assessment with which the author agrees. Rao defines freedom as "a deliberate choice or communication with one another or self-identity or courage of conviction, the fearless expression of one's personality or simply 'being' itself" (92).

If tradition implies accepting repeated abuse and injustice within marriage, then Sahgal's women reject it. If, contrarily, divorce, separation, and seeking fulfillment outside marriage imply modernity, then Sahgal's women opt for it. These women, who walk out of their marriages, obviously require the support system which only a modern civil society can provide. They also need to attain financial independence. This means that they must not face unfair discrimination in the job market. A whole society's acceptance of constitutional safeguards is assumed in this act of divorce. However, the problems of working women in our society are not directly addressed in Sahgal's novels. Sonali, the lone exception, is an Indian Administrative Service officer of the post-Independence generation who takes constitutional safeguards for granted. When she is transferred, it is not because she is a woman but because she does not accept the new culture of the Emergency. Overall, though, insofar as the status of women is concerned, Sahgal comes across as against the tradition inherent in the default mode of Hinduism. She questions patriarchal norms, endorsing a humanistic modernity in place of the oppressions of tradition. She clearly sees virtue not in self-immolation but in rebellion.

However, if the woman is a victim of tradition, from where does she get the courage to rebel? It seems to me that this is a crucial question, one which will force us to qualify the above formulation. Sahgal herself says of Simrit: "[She] is a passive creature to whom things happen. . . . Simrit is not an individual--she is culture, tradition, a patient enduring passivity."(9) If Rashmi, Saroj, and Simrit all represent the traditional Sita type, passive and long-suffering, what does their rebellion signify? It signifies, surely, that even a Sita will not remain forever passive. Even she will rebel when oppression becomes unbearable. Moreover, if Simrit is tradition or culture, then her rebellion means that our tradition must change, must rebel against its evil "Other." In other words, tradition itself must provide the impetus for change by negating those of its aspects which are inimical to its survival.

Hence, though Saroj and Simrit are oppressed by tradition, it is tradition which gives them the strength to rebel. At any rate, it gives them the inner resources to survive, to reach out to modernity, to seek help from the other side, as it were. In fact, the women in Sahgal are always emotionally and spiritually stronger than their husbands. Simrit, for instance, walks out in spite of having an unspecified number of children and being saddled with a crippling financial contract. It seems that this inner strength is very akin to the traditional notion of the woman as Shakti. What Sahgal wishes to say, however, is that Shakti must express herself not through self-immolation but through a demand for equality in the present times.

Politics and Tradition

Tradition invariably seeps into politics in Sahgal. Here tradition acquires positive connotations, as opposed to the negative connotations associated with it in the main plot. Tradition in the subplots usually refers to the Gandhi-Nehru brand of political action, the legacy of the freedom movement.

Sahgal's novels usually begins at a point of transition. The old Gandhi-Nehru brand of politics--is about to be replaced by the new. In *Storm in Chandigarh* and *The Day in Shadow* the old ministers are on the point of death, about to be replaced by a newer, more corrupt, amoral breed of racketeers represented by the likes of Sumer Singh. Even in *This Time of Morning* there is a sustained ideological opposition between Kailas and Kalyan. In this novel Kalyan himself is seen as divided, and in the end his better instincts triumph. In the later novels, though, the split is complete and unbridgeable. The climax of this indictment of the new is reached in *Rich Like Us*. Here Dev,(read Sanjay Gandhi), represents the abuse of power. The old order is represented in Jayaprakash Narayan himself (RLU,46).

The opposition between the old and the new in the politicians is also echoed in the bureaucrats. Sahgal knows that India is governed by politicians and bureaucrats. These are the two tiers of our political and administrative ruling class. A degeneration of our polity will occur only when the rot sets into both these tiers. Hence, the erosion of values of the politicians must be followed by an erosion of values of the bureaucrats. We have several images of the old-style Indian Civil Service officer. He is usually portrayed as a plodder, an obeyer of rules and regulations. He is not imaginative, but he is solid, dependable, and upright. Indeed, his honesty is his chief virtue. Sir Arjun (*This Time of Morning*), Trivedi (*Storm in Chandigarh*), and Keshav (*Rich Like Us*) are prime examples. As opposed to this, the new type of bureaucrat, best exemplified by Ravi Kachru (*Rich Like Us*), is alternately ignorant and opportunistic. All is not lost though; the new generation of bureaucrats also contains Vishal (*Storm in Chandigarh*), Raj (*The Day in Shadow*), and Sonali *(Rich Like Us)*. It is interesting how the latter has to resign from the Indian Administrative Service. The implication is that there is no place for the honest and law-abiding officer in the new regime.

The conflict between tradition and modernity in the political subplots thus privileges tradition over modernity. Tradition represents the positive Gandhian and Nehruvian values of compassion, satyagraha, nonviolence, and social justice, combined with the democratic values of socialism, civil liberties, rule of law, and so on. Modernity is associated with corruption, illegal activities, fascism, political violence, suppression of civil liberties, dictatorship, the politics of the personality cult, and the like. The deterioration in public life is best shown in *Rich Like Us*, set during the Emergency of 1975-77. However, the tradition-modernity question in the subplot has little to do with the lives of the women characters. What is interesting, though, is that all of Sahgal's heroines are instinctively on the side of tradition and the old values in politics. Saroj, Simrit, Devi, Rose, and Sonali are examples.

Still, the two senses of tradition do combine at times. When looking for the causes of the political malaise in India, Sahgal often goes back to Hinduism. Again, she seeks in the prevailing ideology the reasons for our failures. However, her analysis is not facile or naive. She is aware of the complexity of our tradition. As Vishal says in *Storm in Chandigarh:* "We seem to be in the grip of impotence, stuck for answers, because the most effective part of our inheritance isn't brought into play" (SC, 17). It is this part of our inheritance which Gandhi reactivated so effectively, Sahgal would imply. Vishal's discussions with Trivedi and his proposed paper on Brahminism are all a part of his ongoing quest for the answer to the riddle of the Indian character. Where have we gone wrong? Where has our leadership failed? Such questions haunt him. The failures of independent India exasperate him. The disintegration of civil life in Chandigarh is linked to "the funeral march of Hinduism": "History will say, these were a people who couldn't survive modern times. The modern world was too much for them. They never came to terms with it. They just went to pieces. They could have lived if they had the courage . . . to change" (SC, 92). This is an important passage which once again links our political failures with the inertia of tradition. India is seen as a traditional society resistant to change, yet the failure of Sahgal is not the failure of tradition alone but the absence of courage. Courage, of course, belongs to neither tradition nor modernity exclusively. So, once more, the key lies outside the tradition-modernity question in an independent groundwork of values which, to Sahgal, are necessary for our survival and success.

Tradition-Modernity and Personal Relationships:

A final area where the tradition-modernity question operates is personal relationships. This is where, I believe, Sahgal is the most suggestive and allegorical, where her own brand of synthesis is most discernible. By personal relationships I mean the values that characters represent and endorse when they are intimately involved with another person. Again, when we examine the heroines Rashmi, Saroj, Simrit, Devi, Rose, and Sonali, we see a whole web of traditional values being affirmed. I call these values traditional because they are found in the religious traditions of most of the major religions of the world. Thus we see a range of related oppositions: altruism/selfishness, compassion/cruelty, nonviolence/violence, materialism/spirituality, and, above all, love/lovelessness.

To begin with, we may observe that the men, Dalip, Inder, Som, and Ram, are all selfish. They put themselves and their needs, physical, emotional, and material, above those of others. This selfishness reaches pathological proportions in Dev, who is portrayed as a monster. Dev, we should remember, murders his own stepmother. The other men do not go quite so far. The women, both biologically and emotionally, are givers. They long to share themselves with others. They are not totally self-centered. Rather, they are more sensitive to their people's needs. As mothers and housewives, they are almost always attuned to the needs of their children and husbands. Saroj and Simrit, when pregnant, have an almost ecstatic fascination with the new life growing in them. They are life-affirming and loving. Remember Rose's ministrations of the disabled beggar. The husbands, on the other hand, seem to be incapable of love. They have a kink in their characters which substitutes domination for love. Likewise, the women are not materialistic, basically. They value comfort and prosperity but not above emotional and spiritual fulfillment. What happens to Simrit is illustrative. As Som gets richer and richer, he also becomes more, corrupt, and uncaring. He is noticeably dehumanized. Som's wealth comes from making weapons of mass destruction; the violence which he seems to abet in the world outside also returns to destroy his own family life. Inder, too, beats Saroj in the earlier novel. Simrit nearly goes mad in such an atmosphere of material greed and inhumanity.

If one word or category were used to sum up the whole gamut of traditional values which the women endorse, it would be love. In "Passion for India" Sahgal implies that the goal of human relationships is "true everlasting love, . . . real give and take, a love that transcends misunderstanding" (84). The last phrase is actually a play on the biblical notion of peace that "passeth understanding." Of course, it could be argued that love is no more traditional than courage is modern. True, but the kind of love that Sahgal seems to describe is what the religious traditions of the world emphasize; it is a set of values which the machine age of modernity is wont to destroy or suppress.

In brief, the women represent love, charity, compassion, kindness, altruism, and a preference for the emotional over the material. The husbands are selfish, cruel, violent, possessive, and materialistic. The contrast is so old as to be seen in religious terms. The values that the women embody are essentially the core of the ethical and moral code of most religions. I would say that at heart the women are religious and traditional. That is, they believe that nonviolence and compassion and sharing will solve the problems of the world. The men are greedy, materialistic, and violent and therefore represent the unpalatable underbelly of capitalism and modernity. Their actions, multiplied a million fold, by implication result in wars and poverty.

The values of the heroines are thus essentially conservative. As Saroj says, they involve a courage which consists in "not throwing things away, but holding on . . . and never giving up" (SC, 92). This tradition of cultivating virtue is basically idealistic-humanistic in that it refuses to accord primacy to the material. Sonali's critique of Marxism arises from her refusal to submit to the domination of either a Eurocentric world view or a master discourse: "I . . . had no intention of chaining myself to any doctrine when I had just lost some of my chains" (RLU, 101).

Liberal, humanistic, Gandhian, social reform--call it a combination of all these. The prevailing ideology in Sahgal's works thus retains the core of religious values from Hinduism, Buddhism, and Christianity, plus a selective acceptance of essentially bourgeois values from modernity. Essentially, this synthesis consists of the humanistic and spiritual heritage which comes from tradition combined with reformative or heterodox Hinduism and Western liberalism. From the latter, ideas and values like individuality, freedom, and the quest for happiness are accepted. Overall, the package may be called liberal Gandhism.

It was Jain who characterized Sahgal as a person with "the conscience of a liberal and the spirit of a non-conformist" (9). This is an apt definition. Sahgal, in a letter to this writer, says, "I am a conservative (i.e., careful about stepping out into the new) who has been constantly driven to being a revolutionary by the force of circumstances and the nature of events around me."(10) With her privileged family background, she could have attained any high office she might have desired; instead, she has consistently tried to be a "<u>VUP</u>"--a "very unimportant person" (PI, 87). Ultimately, what is significant about Sahgal is not her ideological position, which is liberal bourgeois, but the hardships and trials through which she has sustained this position. That is what makes for its continuing viability and authenticity in our times. Ultimately, it is a judicious mixture of tradition and modernity which constitutes the underlying value system of Sahgal's novels. And at the crux of such a synthesis is usually a female protagonist, the crisis in whose life reflects the crisis in contemporary India.

Nayantara – the insider participant

Are sensibilities gendered? Is gender a result of social conditioning? Have we come to accept knowledge received about gender unconditionally? If so, perhaps we have to reframe knowledge because time and situation does not remain the same. What has prompted this kind of preliminary conclusion is to this book by Nayantara Sahgal, *Indira Gandhi: Tryst with Power.*

Nayantara Sahgal belonged to the innermost circle of the Nehru family. Her mother Vijayalakshmi Pandit was Nehru's closest friend, confidant and most loved sister. Nayantara's access to knowledge about Indira Gandhi was therefore more authentic. She had the inner eye. This does not mean that we take whatever she has to say as unquestionable. Yet she gives us one more version of history, rather Herstory

I am invariably reminded of *Nehru* by Shashi Taroor. If History were to be written in this way then Taroor would have had millions who loved history and those millions would of course be women. Reading Nayantara's *Indira Gandhi* and Taroor's *Nehru*, one is struck by an important element in the writing of history: that of relationships. Nehru's relationship with his father Motilal in Taroor and Indira's relationship with her father in Nehru.

Nayantara's *Indira Gandhi Tryst with Power* is a uniquely written book. If history books were written in this manner, readers would have access to more personal information where the character of people would emerge. Indira Gandhi comes alive as Nayantara comes alive. We become aware of both the minds. In the section titled *The Person* Nayantara describes Indira Gandhi.

> Mrs Gandhi remained for the country a muted figure. A poor speaker and instinctively swift to prevent any encroachments on her position and

prestige, she gave an impression of inhibition and
wariness. (18)

Nehru himself had his misgivings. Sahgal tells us that "…
given the keen awareness Nehru had of his daughter and
the intellectual and emotional labour he expended on her,
he could not bring the cherished child to flower. Somewhere
within, her intensities, locked, and the tight bud stayed
closed…Her unresponsiveness troubled her father during her
adolescence. Indu…seldom lowered her guard." (31) Nehru
felt and experienced the way in which Indira "ignored" him
and others completely. He saw that she lived in a "world
of dreams and vagaries and floats about on imaginary
clouds, full probably of all manner of brave fancies." (31)
He saw that she was "extraordinarily imaginative and self
centered…" (31)

Very interestingly, Nayantara analyses the cause of Indira's
behavior arising from the relationship of her parents, Nehru
and Kamala. Sahgal sees their marriage as a "grievous
mistake" for they were mismatched. They were two
profoundly dissimilar people. Kamala was barely educated
and orthodox, whereas the Nehrus were liberal, emancipated,
and westernized. Since "marriages in which the wife was not
her husband's equal in education or opportunity where the
rule rather than the exception" as Sahgal records, Kamala
had problems in adapting to this new environment and
it built up in symptoms of illness. This left the caring of
Indira in the hands of Nehru, which he did quite admirably
as history has to tell us, but what happened to Indira is
something of a mystery until the publication of her mother's
biography in May 1973 where Indira Gandhi said in an

interview with its author that "her mother had had the greater influence on her. In her teens she had felt her mother was being wronged by her father's family and had fought for her. "I saw her being hurt and I was determined not to be hurt". (38) With her mother always ailing and her father's family always robust and radiating energy, it was perhaps difficult for Indira to distinguish between these two sides. The Nehru's name was a talisman but her trust and instincts were reposed in the simpler, uncritical background of her mother's relations. She also resented the "beautiful, vivacious elder aunt... who occupied a special place in her father's affections" (39) Indira did not encourage family ties after her father's death and her aunts retirement from politics.

Despite all this, very astutely Sahgal is of the opinion that "...simple formulas seldom tell the whole story of family relationship, where the immediate and personal often becomes blurred and mellowed by the larger cushioning of common living and common interests.(40)

After Nehru's death, Indira slowly moved on to be the heir and successor. We understand that Nehru himself had never been overtly agreeable to Indira's position as the Congress President in 1959. "Nehru did not think it was time for this distinction. His reservations were rooted deep in his respect for the process – personal, political, social or economic – that lays sound foundations. Work was the crucible of human personality or political strength, and there were not shortcuts to excellence, a philosophy reflected in seventeen years of power that rejected the dramatic and the extreme and relied on the building of institutions... (yet) He decided not to intervene" (2)

Indira Gandhi's style of functioning was completely different from that of Nehru and flung to the margins all stereotypical behaviours believed to belong to women. "She represented something ruthless and new" (82) says Sahgal speaking about the split of the Congress and the election of the V.V. Giri as the President of India. Indira Gandhi described herself as a "...tough politician." (83) She was "... projected as the agent of historic process, woman of destiny, champion of the poor, in touch with people's urges and aspirations and uniquely qualified to lead them". (83) The resemblance with Nehru was over and one needs to read Sahgal to realize that defining womanhood through Indira Gandhi would be a confusing affair. Nehru had more of the feminine in him, if sympathy, concern and kindness were defined to be the parameters needed to define woman. The relationships of Indira Gandhi with many of her colleagues, were markedly different from what Nehru had. His speeches had a "quality of intimacy" hers "charged the atmosphere with a peculiar tension.(83) Was it because she was a woman and the men in power were not in a position to take in the way she dealt with things? Were the expectations of her being a woman thwarted which led to the confusion? Or did they think wrong? Did they refuse to see her for what she had always been? Nayanatara Sahgal's perceptive reading with all supporting documents of her cousin's attitudes and lifestyle is an eye opener. We see her for what she is and she defies any definition of what it is to be a woman. We need different parameters.

Indira Gandhi has been gone for a long time, yet our fascination with her (and her legacy) endures, and the 1975 Emergency remains a watershed in India's political history.

Indeed, the Emergency was the trigger, Sahgal says, for her book: her attempt was, one, to give voice to the thousands (including herself) who were silenced at the time, either by arrest or intimidation; and two, to offer an account of how one woman could reverse or negate the democratic values which post-Independence India had, by and large, upheld. Nayantara Sahgal shows the effect of personality on history and a different side to woman in politics.

Nayantara had said in an interview

> It is not a biography but a study of her political style... because her style was a definite departure from that of her two predecessors and from the way the Congress party had functioned until then. The book started as a paper I was asked to contribute to a conference on "Leadership in South Asia" at SOAS (School of Oriental & African Studies), London University, in 1974. When my conclusion that we were heading toward authoritarian rule proved to be correct, I expanded it into a book. As a close relative I was able to give it a personal dimension.[27]

"I wrote against my cousin because she was my cousin," Nayantara has said, and because she could not understand how Mrs. Gandhi could systematically dismantle the foundations and institutions of a freedom hard won. But there were other factors, too: Sahgal's growing concern at the decline of the Congress as a national force, post-1969;

---

[27] http://www.thehindu.com/books/indira-and-india/article4058100.ece

Mrs Gandhi's open alliance with the CPI, post-1971; and Nayantara's own solidarity with the JP Movement as a counter to Indira Gandhi's authoritarianism. Not surprisingly, developments around these dates dominate in her telling, with the greatest attention paid to the pre-Emergency period and the Bihar Movement. The Allahabad High Court judgement of June 20, 1975, in her view, followed party reversals in Gujarat, Kerala and Tamil Nadu; while the massive support that JP was able to mobilise in a relatively short time was dangerously unsettling for the PM.

Ritu Menon writes "After Mrs Gandhi's defeat in 1977, a rash of books on her and her political style appeared, but Nayantara Sahgal's is one of the most clear-eyed and critical in its analysis. Her recounting of the lead-in to the Emergency is detailed and unrelenting, illustrating the impact of irresistible force meeting immovable object: two towering personalities – JP and Indira – and their effect on history. There is a third towering personality in this book, and that, of course, is Nehru, whose political legacy the author believes was unforgivably subverted by his daughter. Non-alignment was abandoned by cosying up to the Soviet Union; decision-making by consensus was jettisoned; chief ministers were unseated, Congress cadres were demoralized, an all-encompassing quest for power replaced a visionary politics. Indira Gandhi substituted Nehru's – and India's – tryst with destiny with her individual tryst with power and this, in her cousin's opinion, was her greatest – and gravest – betrayal. Yet, it can be argued that Mrs Gandhi, by nationalizing banks, abolishing the princes' privy purses and increasing state control of the economy was pursuing her version of a Nehruvian socialism, while simultaneously eroding his principles. Decades, and many assessments later, Mrs Gandhi remains something of a paradox, as Sahgal herself concludes in her epilogue – but this by no means cancels out the body blows she dealt to India's political life." (ibid)

Towards A Conclusion

Sahgal is a writer "...who engaged so persistently and creatively with the public life and politics under colonialism and neo-colonialism while revealing the myriad problems of being marginalised by gender, race, age abilities and beliefs" (Joseph, Preface ix). Her writings has evolved commonsensically, yet she managed to represent the implausible performance of the marginalised as resisting and even finding a new life under oppression. According to Joseph, the most defining agency in Sahgal's works are the "human person".

At the risk of investing in 'bad politics" as Joseph says, the focus of my work is also on "the person" albeit in a different manner/perspective. The tenet of woman being a cultural construct is good enough to begin with.

Are women culturally constructed? Is she not a thinking subject? Does the culture create her subject hood or does it destroy? In Sahgal, one encounters the conventional figures of daughter, virgin, wife, mother etc.

Are human beings determined by system and ideologies? Does literature answer and confront these issues? Apparently they seem to do so in Sahgal. Interestingly colonisation, issues of oil in the Middle East, race and patriarchy are some of her concerns.

Her characters emerge against the backdrop of a very crucial time in the history of India. It is under the yoke of colonialism or the threat of neo-colonialism. Such a character who is pushed to the margins by social, cultural or political determination does not cower down but finds alternative ways to self-actualize and find meanings. Her works refuse to suggest that persons are constructed subjects.

The virgin wife in Sahgal is a victim. The demand of virginity renders a woman anonymous within the four walls of her house. Saroj, with her husband, children, housekeeping and pregnancy has no identity beyond that other family.. In *This Time of Morning* Leela, a student in the US breaks traditional taboos, goes out with men but commits suicide when she realises that she is pregnant. She is ideologically conditioned but bravely would resist through death. According to Sherry Ortner, virginity is especially important in hypergamous or upwardly mobile marriages, where the move is always upwards for the woman. Dowry is important but added to dowry is the exclusivity of woman as virgin. She also points out that the imagined elite status of the virgin stands for not the actual status of the family or group but the desired level. Through the virgin, the family moves upward towards the unattainable status and it is this unattainable status that arouses anger and sadism against a woman who goes "astray" (as quoted in Joseph 32) The literary level of representation of such patriarchal ideology is the figuration of the virgin and wife as a victim in Sahgal's novels.

In the elite society that Sahgal describes, the housewife spends most of her time inside the house. When and if she travels, she is before dark and always chauffeured. Rashmi, in *This Time of Morning* defies this. She drives, always alone and refuses to be chauffeured around. But Nita is chauffeured.

The woman's acquaintances and friends should have the approval of her family, most importantly her husband and these friends are invariably connected to his work and she plays the hostess. This is true with Mira in *This Time of Morning* but not acceptable to Rashmi. Saira also falls in line to a certain extent, but she dares to have friends who do not have the approval of her husband.

However. this 'protection' by men could be confinement for women. This becomes clear in *Shadows*. The consent terms of Simrit's divorce to the scrutiny of justice is found severely wanting. The Hindu Code Bill of 1955 had legalised divorce but had several loopholes disadvantageous to women. Simrit compares the consent terms of her divorce to the "consent" of Sati, pointing to the lack of freedom (to consent) as an equal. Confronted by Som's lawyer, Moolchand, Simrit realises the myth of legalities. "What a lie the facts could be, what an appalling lie. Nothing, almost nothing was ever negotiated. Negotiation was a myth – except among equals – and when on earth did equals exist? The side with the bargaining power called the tune, while the others signed on the dotted line."(60) Som is without mercy for Simrit and the court can justify his terms. The impact of the court decision is that Simrit is made to pay her ex-husband's taxes while benefitting from his income. Raj, tries to help Simrit, but finds it difficult to get people to empathise.

> The Republic of India has passed many laws, Simrit my love, but people like N.N.Shah live in it, friendly, God-fearing fellows who wouldn't harm a fly but who can't for the life (of) them see when a woman is bleeding to death with taxes" (146)

The nation protects but also punishes and it is women who are caught in this foul play of patriarchal and national politics. Indira Gandhi was astute enough to see that there was always a wide rift between social laws and actual practice.

It is very clear that in Simrit's case, the focus is on the male, in other words, the intended subject of the nation is male. The female is eclipsed by the male. Raj's conversation with Shah exemplifies this. The divorce settlement is this because the male progeny benefits immensely from it, the mother should be happy. It is only natural that she bears a little inconvenience along the line.

Sahgal's represents Indian society through her women characters as well as the men characters. Her representation takes for granted the active role educated women are expected to play in politics, business, management and economy. However, she equates the possibility of women's professional participation in any sector of activity, and the corresponding possibility of liberation, with the accompanying development of a socialist project for postcolonial India. Due to this, she is able to link the historical processes set in motion with the transition to an independent India to a deep social transformation, which would naturally affect women's condition. Indian postcoloniality thus amounts to an open project, where new roles for women should evolve together with a more general change in Indian mentalities. It is in this sense that one of the main characters, Sonali, remembers her father's vow of confidence on the dawn of independence: "Women like you, are going to Indianise India" (Rich Like Us 28). In this context, it meant that the recreation of an independent Indian identity, free from British colonialism would be created. It also meant that educated trained women were expected to play an important role in the reconstruction of India's renewed identity and more importantly it would not be contained within the domestic sphere. The confluence of colonialism and female oppression makes the formulation of the project of postcolonial future the ground for the liberation of women.

Sahgal's confluence of tradition politics is also responsible for political attitudes, for how a particular culture responds to corruption and the abuse of power. However, in Sahgal's world, politics is an area in which we Indians have our own positive tradition because of the national struggle for independence. This tradition, chiefly, is the combined legacy of Mahatma Gandhi and Jawaharlal Nehru. There is in it the Gandhian emphasis on truth, nonviolence, satyagraha, social justice, prayer, poverty, simplicity, and so on, and the Nehruvian emphasis on socialism, democracy, and progress. In addition, there is a third realm on which the question of tradition and modernity has bearing. This has to do with the values and life-choices of the main characters, especially as they are revealed in intimate relationships. It is necessary to examine how these three kinds of tradition are depicted in Sahgal's novels. Only then can we form some idea of her own brand of synthesis between tradition and modernity.

Bibliography

Primary Sources:

Sahgal, Nayantara *A Time to Be Happy.* New York, Knopf, and London, Gollancz, 1958.

...., *This Time of Morning.* London, Gollancz, 1965; New York, Norton, 1966.

...., *Storm in Chandigarh.* New York, Norton, and London, Chatto andWindus, 1969.

....*The Day in Shadow.* New Delhi, Vikas, 1971; New York, Norton, 1972; London, London Magazine Editions, 1975.

A Situation in New Delhi. London, London Magazine Editions, 1977.

...., *Rich Like Us.* London, Heinemann, 1985; New York, Norton, 1986.

..., *Plans for Departure*. New York, Norton, 1985; London, Heinemann, 1986.

Mistaken Identity. London, Heinemann, 1988; New York, NewDirections, 1989.

Uncollected Short Stories

"The Promising Young Woman," in *Illustrated Weekly of India*(Bombay), January 1959.

"The Golden Afternoon," in *Illustrated Weekly of India* (Bombay), February 1959.

"The Trials of Siru," in *Triveni* (Madras), January 1967.

"The Girl in the Bookshop," in *Cosmopolitan* (London), September, 1973.

"Martand," in *London Magazine*, August-September 1974.

"Crucify Me," in *Indian Horizons* (New Delhi), October 1979.

"Earthy Love," in *Trafika* (Prague), Autumn 1993.

Other

Prison and Chocolate Cake (autobiography). New York, Knopf, andLondon, Gollancz, 1954.

From Fear Set Free (autobiography). London, Gollancz, 1962; NewYork, Norton, 1963.

The Freedom Movement in India. New Delhi, National Council of Educational Research and Training, 1970.

Sunlight Surround You, with Chandralekha Mehta and Rita Dar. Privately printed, 1970.

A Voice for Freedom. New Delhi, Hind, 1977.

Indira Gandhi's Emergence and Style. New Delhi, Vikas and Durham, North Carolina, Academic Press, 1978.

Indira Gandhi: Her Road to Power. New York, Ungar, 1982;London, Macdonald, 1983.

Relationship: Extracts from a Correspondence (with E.N. MangatRai). New Delhi, Kali for Women, 1994.

Point of View: A Personal Response to Life, Literature, and Politics. New Delhi, Prestige, 1997.

Secondary Sources:

Ann, Editor Forfreedom, *Women Out Of History: A Herstory Anthology.* Los Angeles: F 1973

Arora, Neena _Nayantara Sahgal and Doris Lessing: A Feminist *Study in Comparison* New Delhi: Prestige Books, 1991, p. 70.

Banner, Lois W. "On Writing Women's History." Journal Of Interdisciplinary History 2:2:347-58.1971

Bernard Bailyn, "Considering the Slave trade: History and Memory," William and Mary Quarterly, LVIII (January 2001);

Bennet, Judith M. "Feminism and History," *Gender And History* (3):251-272. 1989 Bock, Gisela. "Women's History and Gender History: Aspects of an International Debate," *Gender And History* 1(1):7-30. 1989

Bhatnagar, Manmohan *The Fiction of Nayantara Sahgal* New Delhi, Creative Books, 1996

Bibliography of Indian Writing in English 2 by Hilda Pontes, New Delhi, Concept, 1985.

Brown, Joanne. "Historical Fiction or Fictionalized History? Problems for Writers of Historical Novels for Young Adults." *ALAN Review* 26.1 (1998). 1 March 2010 'http://scholar.lib.vt.edu/ejournals/ALAN/fall98/brown.html'.

Carey, Peter. *True History of the Kelly Gang.* St Lucia, Qld: U of Queensland P, 2000.

Carl N. *Is There A History Of Women?* Oxford: Clarendon Press. 1975

Carroll, Bernice A. "Mary Beard's Woman As A Force In History: a Critique," Berenice A. Carroll, ed., *Liberating Women's History: Theoretical And Critical Essays.* Urbana,

Ill.: University of Illinois Press, 26-41. Originally published in the MASSACHUSSETTS REVIEW 1972.

Clendinnen, Inga. "The History Question: Who Owns the Past?" *Quarterly Essay* 23 (2006): 1-72.

Chew Shirley "Naryantara Sahgal's *Rich Like Us*" Ranjana Ash, *Motherlands*, edited by Susheil Nasta, London, Women's Press, 1992

…, "The Search for Freedom in Indian Women's Writing" in *Motherlands*, edited by Susheil Nasta, London, Women's Press, 1992

Chowdhury, Maithreyee Review http://www.thehindu. com/books/indira-and-india/article4058100.ece

Current, Richard. "Fiction as History: A Review Essay." *Journal of Southern History* 52.1 (1986): 77-90.

Derrida. *Archive Fever.* Chicago: University of Chicago Press, 1995

Grenville, Kate. "History and Fiction." 2007. 19 July 2010 'http://kategrenville.com/The Secret River History%20 and%20Fiction'.

"Interview with Ramona Koval." 17 July 2005. 26 July 2010 'http://www.abc.net.au/rn/arts/bwriting/stories/s1414510.htm'.

Dalal Nergis, Interview in *Times of India Sunday Review* (New Delhi), 30 June 1985

Davidoff, Leonore et al ed. *Gender and History: Retrospect and Prospect*. Blackwell Publishers 2000 Print

Davis, Natalie Zemon. "'Women's HIstory' in Transition: the European," FEMINIST STUDIES 3(3/4):83-103. 1976

Demos, John. "Afterword: Notes from, and About, the History/Fiction Borderland." *Rethinking History* 9.2/3 (2005): 329-35.

Forbes, Geraldine, *Women in Modern India*. The New Cambridge History of India, Cambridge University Press 2012 Print

Fox-Genovese, Elizabeth. "Placing Women's History in History," NEW LEFT REVIEW 33:5-29. 1982

Gordon, Ann D. Mari Jo Buhle, and Nancy Schrom Dye. "The Problem of Women's History," in Bernice A. Carroll, ed., *Liberating Women's History: Theoretical And Critical Essays,* 75-92. Urbana, Ill.: University of Illinois Press.

Gordon, Linda. "What Should Women's Historians Do? Politics, Social Theory, and Women's History," MARXIST PERSPECTIVES 1(Fall): 131-32. 1979

Gordon, Linda. "What's New in Women's History," in DeLauretis, Theresa, ed., *Feminist Studies/Critical Studies.* Madison, University of Wisconsin Press, 55-66. 1986

Harlan, David. "Historical Fiction and the Future of Academic History." *Manifestos for History*. Ed. Keith Jenkins,

Sue Morgan and Alun Munslow. Abingdon, Oxon; N.Y.: Routledge, 2007.

Hartman, Mary S. and Lois Banner, ed., *Clio's Consciousness Raised: New Perspectives On The History Of Women*. New York: Harper, vii-xii. 1974

Hutcheon, Linda. *A Poetics of Postmodernism: History, Theory Fiction*. New York: Routledge, 1988.

Jenkins, Keith, Sue Morgan, and Alun Munslow. *Manifestos for History*. Abingdon, Oxon; N.Y.: Routledge, 2007.

Jasbir Jain *Nayantara Sahgal* New Delhi, Arnold-Heinemann, 1978

…, *Nayantara Sahgal* Jaipur, India, Printwell, 1994

Kelly-Gadol, Joan. "The Social Relation of the Sexes: Methodological Implications of Women's History." SIGNS: JOURNAL OF WOMEN IN CULTURE AND SOCIETY 1(4):809-23. 1976

Kelly, Joan. *Women, History And Theory: The Essays Of Joan Kelly*. Chicago: Chicago University Press. 1985

Kemp, Sandra and Judith Squires ed *Feminisms Oxford Readers* OUP 1997 Print

Kent, Susan Kingsley, *Theory and History: Gender and History* Palgrave Macmillan 2012 Print

Kumar, Radha, "Identity Politics and the Contemporary Feminist Movement" in *Identity Politics and Women Cultural Reassertions and Feminisms in International Perspective,* Valentine M. Moghadam (ed) Westview Press, Boulder, San Francisco, Oxford1994

Lerner, Gerda. "New Approaches to the Study of Women in American History," Journal of Social History 4(4): 33-56. Also in Berenice A. Carroll, ed., *Liberating Women's History: Theoretical and Critical Essays.* Urbana, Ill.: University of Illinois Press, 1976, 26-41.

...,. *The Majority Finds Its Past: Placing Women In History.* New York: Oxford University Press. 1979

Lukács, György. *The Historical Novel.* Lincoln: University of Nebraska Press, 1983.

Lukacs, John Historical Consciousness or the Remembered Past (reprint New York, 1985)

McKenna, Mark. "Writing the Past: History, Literature & the Public Sphere in Australia." *Australian Financial Review* (2005). 13 May 2010 'http://www.afraccess.com.ezp01. library.qut.edu.au/search'.

Menon, Ritu *Out of line: A literary and Political Biography of Nayantara Sahgal* Harper Collins 2015

Narendra, Madhuranthakam *Microcosms of Modern India: A Study of the Novels of Nayantara Sahgal,* New Delhi, Classical Pub. Co., 1998

Nelson, Camilla. "Faking It: History and Creative Writing." *TEXT: Journal of Writing and Writing Courses* 11.2 (2007). 5 June 2010 'http://www.textjournal.com.au'.

Offen, Karin; Ruth Roach Pierson; and Jane Rendall, eds., *Writing Women's History: International Perspectives.* Bloomington, Ind.: Indiana University Press, 45-58. 1991

Pierre Nora, "Between Memory and History: Les Lieux de Memoire, Representations, 26 (Spring 1989): 7 - 25

Paranjape, Makarand "The Crisis of Contemporary India and Nayantara Sahgal's Fiction" in *World Literature Today,* Spring 1994

Rajan, Rajeshwari Sunder, ed. *Signposts – Gender Issues in Post Independence India.* New Brunswich: Rutgers University Press, 2001.

Rao, Krishna A.V. *Nayantara Sahgal: A Study of Her Fiction and Non- fiction 1954-1974* Madras, Seshachalam, 1976

Reimer, Eleanor S., and John C. Fout. "Women's History: Recent Journal Articles," TRENDS IN HISTORY 1(1):3-22. 1979

Ricketson, Matthew. "Not Muddying, Clarifying: Towards Understanding the Boundaries between fiction and Nonfiction." *TEXT: Journal of Writing and Writing Courses* 14.2 (2010). 6 June 2011 'http://www.textjournal.com.au/oct10/ricketson.htm'.

Rosenstone, Robert A. "Space for the Bird to Fly." *Manifestos for History*. Eds. Keith Jenkins, Sue Morgan and Alun Munslow. Abingdon, Oxon; N.Y.: Routledge, 2007. 11-18.

Rowbotham, Sheila. *Hidden From History: Rediscovering Women In History From The 17ᵗʰ Century To The Present*. New York: Pantheon Books. 1975 Degler,

Roy, Kumkum *The Power of Gender and the Gender of Power: Explorations in Early Indian History* OUP 2010 Print

Sangwan, Uplabdhi *Exploring Models of Femininity in Women's Writings* - Journal of Indian English Writers www.indianruminations.com

Schama, Simon. *Dead Certainties: (Unwarranted Speculations)*. 1ˢᵗ Vintage Books ed. New York: Vintage Books, 1992.

Scott, Ann F. "Woman's Place Is in the History Books," in *Making The Invisible Woman Visible*. Urbana, Ill.: University of Illinois, 361-370. 1980-89

Scott, Joan W., *Gender And The Politics Of History*. New York: Columbia University Press. 1984

Slotkin, Richard. "Fiction for the Purposes of History." *Rethinking History* 9.2/3 (2005): 221-36.

Smith-Rosenberg, Carroll. "The New Woman and the New History." FEMINIST STUDIES 3(1/2):171-98. 1976

..., "Hearing Women's Words: A Feminist Reconstruction of History," in *Disorderly Conduct: Visions Of Gender In Victorian America.* New York: Oxford University Press, 11-52. 1986

..., "Writing History: Language, Class, and Gender," in Teresa de Lauretis, ed., FEMINIST STUDIES/CRITICAL STUDIES. loomington, Ind: Indiana University Press, 32-54. 1986

Southgate, Beverley C. *History Meets Fiction.* New York: Longman, Harlow, England, 2009.

Scott, Joan W. Gender: A Useful Category of Historical Analysis *The American Historical Review*, Vol. 91, No. 5. (Dec., 1986), pp. 1053-1075.http://links.jstor.org/sici?sici=0002-8762%28198612%2991%3A5%3C1053%3AGAUCOH%3E2.0.CO%3B2-Z

Talwar, Sree Rashmi *Woman's Space: The Mosaic World of Margaret Drabble and Nayantara Sahgal* S New Delhi, Creative Books, 1997

The Polity Reader in Gender Studies Polity Press 2002 Print

Uraizee, Joya *This Is No Place for a Woman: Nadine Gordimer, Nayantara Sahgal, Buchi Emecheta, and the Politics of Gender* Trenton, New Jersey, Africa World Press, 1999

White, Hayden. "Introduction: Historical Fiction, Fictional History, and Historical Reality." *Rethinking History* 9.2/3 (2005): 147-57.